The Corporate
Speech Writer's
Handbook

Recent Titles from Quorum Books

The Corporate Speech Writer's Handbook

A GUIDE
FOR PROFESSIONALS IN
BUSINESS, AGENCIES,
AND THE
PUBLIC SECTOR

Jerry Tarver

QUORUM BOOKS

NEW YORK • WESTPORT, CONNECTICUT • LONDON

Library of Congress Cataloging-in-Publication Data

Tarver, Jerry, 1934-
   The corporate speech writer's handbook.

   Bibliography: p.
   Includes index.
   1. Speechwriting.   I. Title.
PN4142.T36   1987   808.5'1   86-30269
ISBN 0-89930-227-0 (lib. bdg. : alk. paper)

Library of Congress Catalog Card Number: 86-30269
ISBN: 0-89930-227-0

First published in 1987 by Quorum Books

Greenwood Press, Inc.
88 Post Road West, Westport, Connecticut 06881

Printed in the United States of America

The paper used in this book complies with the
Permanent Paper Standard issued by the National
Information Standards Organization (Z39.48-1984).

10   9   8   7   6   5   4   3   2

To the participants
in my seminars,
who taught me more
than I taught them.

"Then the conclusion is obvious, that
there is nothing shameful in the mere
writing of speeches. But in speaking
and writing shamefully and badly, instead of as one should, that is where
the shame comes in."

Socrates, in Plato's *Phaedrus*

Contents

Introduction

> If speech writing can become an acquired art, with art's objective of
> reducing form and substance to their simplest and most effective terms,
> our people will rise up as a body in grateful appreciation.
>
> —Freshley (1965, 105)

After many years of working with hundreds of speech writers in government and business, I have concluded that the role of the speech writer is
often not well understood. The executives who need the services of a speech
writer and the managers who direct the communications programs in which
a writer works frequently demand too much, in too short a time, and with
too little guidance. As a result, the novice speech writer is often tossed into
troubled waters and told to sink or swim.

I hope that this book will be of practical value to professional speech
writers. I have two specific objectives in mind. First, I will explain the basic
principles to follow in getting down on paper words that are to be heard
rather than read. I will discuss, with examples, the techniques that writers
need, techniques that are not always the same as the ones that produce good
reports, articles, or essays. The techniques I present here are those that
make speech writing an art that can be acquired.

For experienced writers who examine this book, study of these techniques
will take the form of a review, an opportunity to rethink the principles on
which successful practice is based. Established writers may not agree with
every idea encountered here, but the book should provide the occasion for a
systematic examination of the fundamentals of speech writing. For less

experienced writers, I hope the techniques will offer practical guidance that will help get the next speech written competently and confidently.

My second objective is to discuss speech writing as a profession. Speech writers need to be fully aware of the tradition behind their work. They need to be concerned about the status of speech writing and to tackle typical problems that arise in their work. Because writers of speeches often have little contact with others engaged in the same endeavor, they may not realize that many of the difficulties they struggle to overcome are also encountered by large numbers of their fellow writers. I hope the material on professional issues will be regarded as practical rather than merely incidental. I believe that the quality of a writer's work depends in part on the writer's sense of self-worth and professional pride.

Parts of this book are directed specifically to meeting the first objective. Chapters on content, structure, and language provide useful writing techniques. Other parts of the book primarily support the second objective. For instance, chapter 1 on the speech writer as a professional communicator places speech writing in historical perspective and brings out into the open many of the problems that make speech writing a challenging job. Chapter 2 on building a productive speaker-writer relationship deals in equal measure with matters of professional interest and with techniques that will help writers produce better speeches. Writers interested in studying speech writing in more depth will find the Bibliography a helpful guide.

For the writer who picks up this book as a first-aid kit for a speech already underway, a glance at the chapter titles will suggest which topics should be taken up immediately and which can be deferred. Such a writer might be able to find some practical advice by skimming through chapter 2 on the speaker-writer relationship. The writer could then move on to chapter 3 on audience and objectives, to chapter 4 on organization of ideas, to chapter 5 on content, and to chapter 6 on language. Then the writer could determine if useful information is to be found in chapter 7 on humor or chapter 8 on coaching the speaker in speech delivery. After the writing assignment has been completed, the writer could return to chapter 1 on the history and status of speech writing as a profession, to chapter 10 on special types of speeches, and to chapter 11 on the role of speeches in a communications program.

Before turning to writing techniques and to matters of professional interest, two preliminary questions deserve consideration: why read a speech, and what are the ethical considerations?

WHY READ A SPEECH?

Powerful arguments can be made against the desirability of reading a speech from a manuscript. A speaker's contact with an audience suffers when a speech is read. The need to follow the manuscript limits the speaker's ability to look at listeners, and if the speaker does look, little can be done to adapt to any reactions that may be observed. Speakers who depart from their texts in order to adjust to audience response usually find it difficult to make a smooth return to their prepared remarks. Also, most speakers do not read well. Their voices tend to be monotonous and artificial. Emphasis can easily be misplaced, and often it appears to an audience that a speaker reading a manuscript lacks a firm grasp of the ideas being presented.

There exists a long-standing belief in our society that spontaneous remarks are more trustworthy than a calculated statement. Common sense does not support this prejudice; we all know of cases where inaccurate information was blurted out under pressure when the truth would have been told if time had allowed the preparation of a position paper. And certainly we recognize that information presented on the spur of the moment does not have the probable accuracy of that carefully researched for a manuscript speech. But there remains, however unjustified it may be, what R. C. Jebb long ago identified as the "habitual presumption" that "speech is extemporary" (Jebb 1876, lxxi-ii).

Consider these objections in the light of the time and expense involved in manuscript preparation, and we are fully entitled to ask, "Why read a speech?" Some thoughtful answers can be supplied to the question.

First, speeches do not have to be read poorly. President Ronald Reagan is one of the better examples of a speaker with the skill to handle a manuscript well. Any executive who does not have the time to research and organize a speech well enough to give it from notes may have the time to collaborate on the writing and learn the material thoroughly enough to speak intelligently. The speech writer may become a speech coach. Far too many writers have suffered from seeing their speeches murdered by an ill-prepared speaker. In many cases, the job description of the speech writer can justifiably be expanded to include seeing the speech through to delivery. Furthermore, good delivery is a relative matter. Perhaps a speaker who falls short of being an accomplished presenter of manuscripts would fare even worse in speaking extemporaneously. The manuscript might be the lesser of two evils.

A second argument for manuscript speaking may be found in the advantages of precise wording this form of speaking permits. The manuscript allows careful advance study of language. Nuances of meaning can be considered and ideas sharply defined. Failure to word ideas with care can lead to disaster. Years ago, the political career of George Romney was dealt a deadly blow when he stated in a press conference that he had been "brainwashed." Surely he would have been better off with a prepared statement.

The noted preacher, Harry Emerson Fosdick, believed firmly in writing out his sermons word for word. He warned of the dangers of preaching without first committing words to paper: "monotonous style, a limited vocabulary with few synonyms, [and] repetitious ruts of thought." In an interview Fosdick explained:

Writing forces careful consideration of phraseology; makes the preacher weigh his words; compels him to reread what he has written and criticize it without mercy; constrains him to clear up obscurities in thought and language; begets discontent with repetitious mannerisms; and allows the preacher, before he mounts the pulpit, to listen, as it were, to his own sermon as a whole. (McGlon 1954, 51)

The matter of precision extends to the time limit. Most audiences quickly lose interest in a speech that goes overtime. A speaker talking from notes or off the cuff may easily go past the time limit or may use up the allotted time on only a portion of the material that should be covered. Writers who know a speaker's typical rate of speaking can easily guarantee that the speech will end on time.

Some good speakers may choose not to read the manuscript, instead using it as the basis for a successful speech from notes. Such speakers usually benefit from the writer's pattern of organization, they will depend on the writer's research for their evidence, and they occasionally pick up key phrases from the written speech. John F. Kennedy followed this practice in some of his political campaigns. He departed so often from the manuscript released to the press that reporters joked he was a "text deviate."

WHAT ARE THE ETHICAL CONSIDERATIONS?

Ernest Bormann has compared the practice of speech writing to cheating on an exam or rigging a quiz show. Arguing that "deception is inherent" in speech writing, Bormann accepts the idea that a speaker can legitimately be helped in preparing a speech, but he insists that "at some point on the continuum of collaboration the place is reached where the speech changes character" (Bormann 1961a: 263, 266-67). At that point, Bormann insists, speech writing has become unethical.

Donald Smith points out in rebuttal, however, that Bormann's comparison of speech writing with cheating on a test deals with two quite different types of activity (D. Smith 1961, 114). Students taking tests are supposed to be demonstrating what they have learned. Few observers would assume that to be the purpose of a business executive or a political figure giving a speech.

But Bormann does raise issues that need to be considered. If you write a speech for someone else to deliver, are you engaging in deception? If so, is your activity unethical?

Smith argues there is no deception because the presence of speech writers is well known. He claims it would require an "aggressive level of ignorance" for a citizen of the United States not to know that the president has a staff of speech writers. There is no denying, however, that the work of speech writers is treated, if not deceptively, then at least discreetly. As critics point out, the effectiveness of most speeches would be hampered by an announcement at the end stating, "I wish to close with an expression of appreciation for the work of my speech writer on this talk."

In spite of Smith's point about the president, there will often be cases where the audience does not know that the speaker was assisted by a writer. This leads to the consideration of a more fundamental issue: why should we assume there is anything wrong with the writer's help even though that help is kept secret? So long as we are not talking about the case of a student being tested on speaking skills, we have no reason to question the ethics of a corporate or political speaker who calls on a writer for help.

Such people should be permitted or even encouraged to draw on the best advice available in all their activities. The president of the United States, for example, may well advocate a foreign policy or an economic program based on the ideas of others. We judge the quality of the president's mind and character by the worth of the synthesis we find in the final product. We would hardly call a presidential speech distorted because the president failed to credit each adviser for the part that person played in arriving at the policy. The act of stating the policy in public makes the ideas the president's policy just as the act of saying the speech in public makes the words the president's speech.

It would be odd to argue that any speaker entitled to use advisers for ideas and arguments must be compelled to phrase those ideas and arguments with no help. For example, how could we claim that the president of a corporation could ethically adopt a new product or a design recommended by someone else and then not be allowed any aid in describing the product in a speech to the company stockholders? In such a case, the president might or might not have expertise in product design and might or might not have a high degree of skill in preparing a speech. But in either making decisions or making speeches, executives should not be assumed to be working in a vacuum.

A good speech often is the result of a team effort. Just as the speaker uses ideas and language of the writer, the writer may well need to turn to other experts in the organization for help. Good writers often develop a network of advisers and in many cases must rely extensively on data supplied by others.

If deception involves nothing more than failing to give the speech writer public credit, there seems to be no ethical problem. But suppose the deception extends to distorting public perception of a speaker. Is a speech writer engaged in an unethical practice when making a speaker appear more intelligent, more articulate, or wittier than the speaker would be if the speaker prepared the talk without help? Suppose, for example, that a speech writer makes a speaker sound witty when in fact the speaker is not. This ethical dilemma is not nearly as likely to occur as some might imagine. Making silk purses out of sows' ears is as difficult as it ever was; an unwitty speaker will not turn into a comedy genius at the hands of a clever speech writer. But even if a writer does improve the level of the speaker's humor, the act of supplying help could hardly be called unethical. Most people who are witty borrow at least some of their material. Who would claim that repeating a joke from *Reader's Digest* was unethical because a person failed to cite the source?

The same analysis can be applied to the writer who makes a dull speaker somewhat more interesting, a verbose speaker a bit more concise, or a rambling speaker better organized. Speech writers work from the same premise as Bormann and the rest of the speech teachers in the field of education: a poor speaker can be improved. If a speaker did not manage to learn the effective use of language or methods of organization, a speech writer supplies the missing skill in the same way that accountants, lawyers, and engineers supply a business or political figure with ideas or procedures the speaker might not have learned.

Although it is easy to conjure up the image of a speaker mouthing the words of a brilliant speech without understanding what is being said, this situation is not likely to occur often. And, of course, some busy speakers could, if they had the time, write their own speeches as well as or better than a speech writer.

We encounter a more difficult problem when an assignment demands that a writer defend a position that the writer does not personally support. In such situations, many speech writers feel they play the role of the advocate. Like lawyers, they are hired to make the best possible case for a client no matter whether they themselves believe in the cause.

It may never be possible to develop an ethical code of conduct that all speech writers could support. In an ideal situation, there would be no ethical problems if the speaker knows and approves the content of the speech and if both the speaker and the writer believe the speech is honest. In short, the goal should be that both the speaker and the writer understand and believe in the speech.

In the case of an important speech in which the speaker is heavily involved in the preparation of the message, the speaker will routinely understand and believe what the speech says. In minor speeches, such as speeches of welcome or a speech presenting an award, a quick glance at the manuscript the day before delivery may be enough to guarantee that the speaker grasps and accepts the ideas.

The rule of common understanding and belief will sometimes be violated. A writer may prepare a glowing tribute to a retiring executive who was strongly disliked by the writer and the speaker. A corporate executive may deliver a speech in support of a company policy the executive has been forced to accept. In short, writers and speakers will occasionally tell the same sorts of white lies that most of us resort to when we say "you're looking well' to a sick friend in need of cheering up.

The speech writer's major ethical problem is not created by the fact that one person is writing a speech for another person. The truly serious ethical questions come in asking whether the information is accurate, the position logical, and the program in the best interest of the audience. And these are questions that have nothing to do with who wrote the speech.

A writer—or a speaker—who invents or distorts a quotation is dishonest. A writer or a speaker who knowingly defends a position not supported by the evidence is practicing deceit. A writer or a speaker who distorts statistics, twists facts, or in any way makes the worse appear the better cause is behaving in unethically.

Almost any issue a speech addresses has two sides. What is right may be relative. Two honest and intelligent people may disagree strongly about what is true or correct. Speakers and speech writers have the ethical responsibility to tell the truth as they see it.

CONCLUSION

Speech writing is a challenging task. It is both craft and art. Its techniques may be learned, but it depends for its success on the talent and sensitivity of the individual writer.

The Corporate
Speech Writer's
Handbook

1

The Speech Writer as a Professional Communicator

Those who had no leisure or taste to become rhetoricians now began to find it worth while to buy their rhetoric ready made.

—Jebb (1876, 1:3)

Many people think that speech writing developed as an outgrowth of modern public relations. In fact, professional speech writing has been around for centuries. No one knows who first prepared a speech for pay. Maybe an early cave dweller, after winning community leadership by brute strength, found it necessary to purchase a few well-spaced grunts to utter at the feast celebrating the success of the autumn pig hunt. Or perhaps an ancient pharaoh hired a grand vizier to write state speeches and compose royal prayers to the sun god.

The Bible documents one remarkable early case. When the Lord instructed Moses to tell the people of Israel to leave Egypt, Moses declined with the excuse, "I am not eloquent . . . but I am slow of speech, and of a slow tongue." As the story develops in chapter 4 of the Book of Exodus, the Lord finally lost patience with Moses and chose Aaron to deliver the message with the explanation, "I know that he can speak well." But Moses was made Aaron's speech writer when he was told "thou shalt speak unto him, and put words in his mouth."

SPEECH WRITER IN CLASSICAL GREECE

By the time Greek civilization was flourishing near the end of the fifth century B.C., speech writers were operating as a recognized profession in the city of Athens. Among the more famous of the speech writers, or logographers, to use the Greek term, was Demosthenes. In addition to being the most eloquent orator of his time, Demosthenes won recognition in his early years as a prolific and highly paid writer of speeches for others.

The most famous teacher of speech in ancient Greece was Isocrates. He competed for pupils with Aristotle and Plato and at the start of his career was known to have composed speeches for pay. Another speech writer of ancient times, Aspasia, helped Pericles write his speeches. She is reputed to have given advice on the best known of the addresses of Pericles, his eloquent Funeral Oration.

One popular logographer of the fifth century B.C., Lysias, recouped a family fortune with large fees he was able to command for his skill in writing speeches. He was best known for his ability to vary his writing style to suit each of his clients. R. C. Jebb gives an interesting account of the work of Lysias:

Although on a few occasions he himself came forward as a speaker, the business of his life was to write for others. All sorts of men were among his clients: all kinds of causes in turn occupied him. . . . If he had been content to adopt the standard which he found existing in his profession, he would have written in nearly the same style for all these various ages and conditions. He would have treated all these different cases upon a uniform technical system, merely seeking, in every case alike, to obtain the most powerful effect and the highest degree of ornament by applying certain fixed rules. Lysias was a discoverer when he perceived that a purveyor of words for others, if he would serve his customers in the best way, must give the words the air of being their own. He saw that the monotonous intensity of the fashionable rhetoric—often ludicrously unsuited to the mouth into which it was put—was fatal to real impressiveness; and, instead of lending to all speakers the same false brilliancy, he determined to give to each the vigour of nature. It was the desire of treating appropriately every case entrusted to him, and of making each client speak as an intelligent person, without professional aid, might be expected to speak under such circumstances, which chiefly determined the style of Lysias. (Jebb 1876, 1:159-60)

Significance of Speech Writing

The Greek period in the history of speech writing offers three interesting insights into the logographer's art.

First, speech writing filled an important need. Greek law did not allow for the hiring of lawyers. Thus citizens who had to go before the courts, either to defend themselves or to bring charges against someone else, had to state their own cases. No law, however, forbade the purchase of a prepared address to be memorized and recited. Many citizens facing a day in court naturally turned to experts for help. Although the details are not fully preserved, the writers sometimes offered their clients advice on legal strategy and may have helped with the rehearsal of the speeches.

The critical role speech writers played did not necessarily win them high regard from society. The logographers did not, for example, have the high status of the sophists, the teachers who taught students, among other things, how to prepare and deliver their own speeches, a subject the Greeks called rhetoric. Although Plato criticized the sophists harshly, they were popular and well paid. The speech writers on the other hand, while rewarded financially, were held in such low esteem that both Demosthenes and Isocrates were embarrassed in later years by their labors as logographers. Whatever social stigma might have been attached to speech writing, the demand for the writer's services remained high.

Although the writers did not have the prestige that the Greeks accorded the teachers, both groups employed the techniques of rhetoric taught in the schools. The second lesson to be learned from a look at the classical logographers is that then, as now, speech writers possessed valuable technical knowledge about the process of communication. Without denigrating the natural talent so useful in preparing or delivering a speech, it can be seen from the Greek experience that the techniques of speech preparation found in such books as Aristotle's *Rhetoric* could be put to practical use. The writers learned how to discover convincing arguments, organize them clearly, and express them appropriately.

Any Greek citizen with the leisure and taste to do so could enroll in one of the schools to learn how to speak effectively. Training was readily available from the sophists who traveled from city to city offering their instruction in rhetoric and other subjects. Although Plato attacked rhetoric heatedly in some of his early dialogues, Aristotle finally brought the teaching of rhetoric into the Platonic Academy. The coexistence of the schools of rhetoric with the practice of speech writing brings us to the third conclusion to be drawn from the success of the logographers: they demonstrated the value of specialization. Learning how to write a good speech could take years of study and experience. Those who chose to put their energies into other pursuits could turn to skilled professionals on those occasions when help was needed.

Decline of the Art

Speech writing faded in importance as the Athenian democracy passed and the Roman dictatorship became the seat of power. Some have argued that the art of speech making, and one might assume the art of speech writing as well, thrives in a relatively free society but declines when decisions are made by authority rather than by free choice.

Perhaps a better explanation for the change that occurred with the growth of Roman power was the increasing importance of the Roman lawyer. Roman society witnessed a bonding of skills in law, speech, and politics that was to recur throughout history.

Speech writing was not totally absent in Rome, but the only speech writers of note were on the payroll of the emperors. When Nero took power on the death of Claudius, he delivered a funeral oration written by Seneca. Seneca also supplied later material for Nero. Another emperor, Otho, employed Trachalus to aid in the preparation of his speeches.

PRESIDENTIAL SPEECH WRITERS

Other cases of speech writing might be cited from ancient history, but after the classical Greek period, the next most important chapter in the history of speech writing is found in the story of the presidency of the United States. Although today's role for the White House speech writer was not created until the election of Franklin D. Roosevelt, several early presidents used the services of others in preparing speeches and public papers.

The first was George Washington. When it was discovered after Washington's death that he had been helped extensively by Alexander Hamilton in writing his Farewell Address, this startling information was kept secret for fifty years. At last the whole story came out, and it was revealed that a first draft of the address was written, at Washington's request, by James Madison. That draft was composed near the end of Washington's first term before he decided to serve another four years. As his second term drew to a close, Washington rewrote the Madison document and sent it to Hamilton, who in effect constructed an entirely new speech.

Washington edited the Hamilton version extensively for style but kept most of the ideas and much of the language. One of Hamilton's chief contributions was to remove a tone of petulance an angry Washington had at first included. Although the address was never delivered, it found its way to the public through newspaper publication and became one of the most famous documents in United States history. Most of the credit should go to a writer whose contribution was unknown until many years after his death.

Abraham Lincoln sought advice in preparing a major speech. When he began to write his first inaugural address, he turned to several important speakers and political leaders. William H. Seward proposed some thirty-six changes in Lincoln's draft. These changes included two passages to replace the original ending of the speech. Lincoln discarded one of Seward's passages but chose to retain and revise the other. The revision shows Lincoln's skill as editor and as speaker in his desperate attempt to calm a divided nation on the eve of civil war:

Seward's Draft	**Lincoln's Revision**
I close. We are not, we must not be, aliens or enemies, but fellowcountrymen and brethren. Although passion has strained our bond of affection too hardly, they must not, I am sure they will not be broken.	I am loath to close. We are not enemies, but friends. We must not be enemies. Though passion may have strained, it must not break our bonds of affection.

| The mystic cords which, proceeding from so many battlefields and so many patriot graves, pass through all the hearths in this broad continent of ours, will yet harmonize in their ancient music when breathed upon by the guardian angel of the nation. | The mystic chords of memory, stretching from every battlefield and patriot grave, to every living heart and hearthstone, all over this broad land will yet swell the chorus of the Union, when again touched, as surely they will be, by the better angels of our nature. |

President Andrew Johnson, whose wife taught him to read and write, found it useful to employ writers in the preparation of some of his speeches and veto messages. Johnson's habit of making rash and belligerent remarks when speaking off the cuff suggests that he should have used speech writers more often.

The assistance given to nineteenth-century presidents of the United States in the preparation of their speeches does not, of course, compare in extent or method to modern practices. In the examples cited, advice was not sought in a systematic way, and advisers were orators and politicians rather than professional writers. The informality of the process may be seen in the story of Daniel Webster helping President James Polk prepare his inaugural address. Much of Webster's valuable advice was rejected. About all he was able to do was to persuade the President to eliminate some of his dull and obscure classical references. As Webster told his friends, he had been successful only in killing off a few Roman senators in the speech.

INFLUENCE OF WHITE HOUSE WRITERS

The cases of Washington, Jackson, Polk, and Lincoln are presented to show that speech writing in the United States has a history reaching well back before the start of the twentieth century. Speech writing in the modern White House is of interest, however, for another reason: the role played by modern presidential speech writers has been responsible to a large degree for the growing importance of speech writing today. The influence of the White House writers is clear in the increasing acceptability of the speech writing function by a huge number of business and government speakers. The White House model can even be said to have had an impact beyond the boundaries of the United States.

The chief effect of the work of presidential speech writers has been a vastly increased public awareness of the speech writing process. The press, which generally appreciates the importance of the role of speech writers, willingly reports their activities to the public, and White House writers in modern times have not been reticent to talk about their work. In two articles in the *Atlantic*, James Fallows gave an inside view of speech writing under President Jimmy Carter (Fallows 1979). William Safire offered fascinating tidbits about life as a speech writer for Richard Nixon in his book, *Before the Fall* (Safire 1975).

At the height of the Iranian hostage crisis, a network television reporter casually turned the spotlight on the role of the speech writer with the comment, "We are expecting a major announcement very soon; we've just seen the President's head speech writer go into the White House."

A more detailed example of the extent to which presidential speech writers are in the public eye can be found in a long article on Richard Nixon's speech writers published the day before Nixon delivered his First Inaugural Address. "The Men behind Nixon's Speeches" by William Honan appeared in the *New York Times Magazine* on January 19, 1969, and gave a complete account of the contributions to various Nixon speeches by Raymond Price, William Safire, Patrick Buchanan, and William Gavin. The article discussed private arguments among the writers over language and strategy. Specific phrases supplied to Nixon by members of the writing team were cited. Readers were encouraged to listen to the coming inaugural for nuances revealing the "rhetorical fingerprints" of each of the Nixon writers. Although the tone of the article was sometimes condescending toward both Nixon and the writers, the story gave the writers full public credit for their work. Such credit contrasts sharply with the embarrassment surrounding the discovery of Hamilton's hand in Washington Farewell Address.

The publicity focusing on the practice of speech writing at the highest political level has contributed to the legitimization of the speech writing process. Lesser political figures as well as corporate executives are able to say, in effect, "If it's good enough for the president of the United States, it's good enough for me."

Merely knowing about the presence of speech writers in the Executive Office Building in Washington does not fully account for the impact of the White House writers. Speeches have been of crucial importance in the leadership of U.S. presidents, and public knowledge of the involvement of speech writers in major addresses has made clear the value of speech writing for any speaker who wishes to be effective.

Ronald Reagan became president because of his ability in public speaking. If he had not made a major campaign address for Barry Goldwater in his unsuccessful bid for the presidency, Reagan would never have become governor of California and thus a serious contender for the presidency. But even Reagan, who has earned by his own efforts his title of the Great Communicator, is known to draw on speech writers for some of his most successful speech material.

Ron Rosenbaum writing in *Esquire* revealed the role of writer Peggy Noonan in supplying some of Reagan's most eloquent words (Rosenbaum 1985, 242-51). The article reports the genesis of dramatic lines from the President's widely acclaimed speech on the fortieth anniversary of the Normandy invasion. Noonan discussed with a presidential advance man the details of the battlefield where the President would speak. As she envisioned Reagan addressing the veterans invited to the occasion, she composed for him the lines, "These are the boys of Pointe du Hoc. These are the men who took the cliffs." Rosenbaum gave Noonan credit also for a quip Reagan made when he gave a radio address shortly after surgery. In reference to Congress and the budget, he said that he wanted to send his doctor to Capitol Hill "to do some cutting."

Attention given to the White House writers, then, makes it hard to ignore the fact that speech writing is acceptable for important speeches and speech writers provide a valuable service. The roster of presidential speech writers has included a number of individuals whose counsel has been valued and whose skills have been appreciated. In addition to the members of the Nixon team already mentioned, other well-known writers in recent years have been McGeorge Bundy, Arthur Schlesinger, Jr., and Theodore Sorensen, who wrote for John F. Kennedy. President Ford reorganized the speech writing staff he inherited from Nixon, and in 1976 he named Robert Orben as his head writer. Orben had been a top writer of professional humor for such personalities as Red Skelton and Dick Gregory, and he also had experience writing speeches for political figures and corporate executives.

Although Adlai Stevenson did not win election to the White House, his race for the office brought out the speech writing talents of poet Archibald MacLeish, historian Bernard deVoto, and playwright Robert Sherwood. Two vice-presidents whose speech writers have gone public are Spiro Agnew and Nelson Rockefeller.

The most famous, and the most unlikely, speech writer in the twentieth century was Dwight Eisenhower. Although Eisenhower was notorious for the twisted syntax of his presidential news conferences, he had demonstrated considerable speaking skill before his entry into politics and had in fact been a speech writer for General Douglas MacArthur. As a member of MacArthur's staff in the 1930s, Eisenhower contributed to MacArthur's speeches and wrote many of his letters as well.

INTERNATIONAL VIEW OF SPEECH WRITING

The practice of speech writing in Great Britain has always been more circumspect than has been the case in the United States. A study by J. Jeffrey Auer revealed that the average British citizen is not aware of the role of speech writers in English politics and business (Auer 1981, 15). Although Prime Minister Margaret Thatcher employed Patrick Cosgrave as her speech writer, the public spotlight did not fall on Cosgrave the way it frequently has on White House writers.

Based on information I have gathered conducting speech writing seminars in England and Scotland, a significant amount of speech writing takes place at the corporate level in Britain. The multinational corporation serves as an efficient conduit in spreading North American habits to other countries.

Not a great deal of information is made public about speech writing in the

Far East. Japanese executives speaking in the United States have adopted American practices to some degree. At the political level, Robert Oliver for many years was a speech writer for officials in the Korean government.

The great bulk of speech writing occurs not at the highest reaches of government but at lower levels of politics or bureaucracy and at the executive level in corporations. A vast number of speech writers work for such figures as ministers of Canadian provinces or governors of states in the United States. In business, the chief executive officers, the presidents, and the vice-presidents of large companies call on their communication departments for speeches.

THE SPEECH WRITER

There is perhaps no such thing as a typical speech writing job. The conditions under which speech writers work and the variety of tasks they perform make it almost impossible to describe the field. Exceptions exist for almost any general statement, but a few tentative observations may offer some insight into the nature of the speech writing profession.

People become speech writers by accident. Almost no one who writes speeches for pay will claim to have started out with such a career in mind. A survey of speech writers for governors in the United States shows that 29 percent of the writers who responded did their academic work in journalism (Freshley 1965, 97). Another survey found journalism backgrounds for 49 percent of the speech writers in corporations examined and for 41 percent of the public relations firms questioned (Baskin 1974, 7).

A career change from journalism to speech writing—or, as is often the case, a career expansion to include speech writing as well as journalism— seems to come about when the right skills happen to be in the right place at the right time. Reporters covering political affairs become involved with politicians as press aides and drift into writing speeches. Or the route from journalism to government may be through work in an advertising or public relations agency. In the corporate world, someone with a journalism background hired to write and edit company publications may be called on to handle a speech writing assignment.

John Ott, in his book *How to Write and Deliver a Speech,* explained how the process worked in his case. On the day his boss was looking for someone to write a company speech, Ott was the only person in the communications office not working on another project. Although he was a writer for the company magazine and had never written a speech, he got the job. He did it well, and the demand for his new-found talent grew. He was soon the company speech writer (Ott 1976, 7-8).

Journalism is not the only avenue to speech writing. Some writers have academic backgrounds in English (2 percent in the Freshley study), while other studied such fields as speech, history, political science, or economics.

Increasingly writers are being sought among the ranks of those with technical backgrounds in, for instance, computers or engineering.

Few communicators are hired specifically for the task of speech writing unless they have had experience. As the Ott incident suggests, this experience often comes about by chance as individuals stumble into speech writing assignments and either do the job well enough to be called on again or fail and fall from the ranks.

Seldom a Full-Time Task

Only a handful of writers work exclusively on speeches. In his study, Baskin found that of employees in corporations who could be identified as speech writers, only 20 percent considered speech writing to be significant enough in their work to identify it as a specialty. In the public relations firms he examined, only 5 percent of those who wrote speeches called themselves specialists (Baskin 1974, 4).

In one of the most extensive surveys made of the speech writing profession, Janine Lichacz (1980) discovered barely 11 percent of the speech writers she contacted spent substantially more than 75 percent of their time on speech writing duties. Nearly a third of her sample worked at speech writing only about 10 percent of their time. Nine writers out of ten in the Lichacz survey worked in the corporate world, as revealed by the additional duties they reported: public relations management, employee communications, press relations, and work on the company annual report.

Working for More Than One Speaker

Just as writers seldom work full time on speeches, they do not often write for only one speaker. Quite commonly a writer can be expected to produce speeches for several top officers. Adjusting to the demands of several bosses can be difficult. In one unfortunate situation, a writer handled the speeches for both the president of the company and the chief executive officer. These two officers were rivals for prestige, and their competition extended to the quality of their speeches. The writer was whipsawed between them as one and then the other demanded more and better speeches.

In a large bureaucracy or a major company, writers may operate in a pool. They are assigned to write for various speakers or to work on nonspeech tasks on the basis of availability and interests. Such an arrangement often includes the availability of a research staff to aid in gathering data. The danger of burn-out is reduced because of the contact with other writers, the variety of job assignments, and the availability of staff support.

Some writers occasionally find they are required to produce pattern talks for speakers' bureau speakers. These speeches, intended as models for bureau members, may be distributed from company headquarters to branches far away. There they are delivered by speakers the writer has never met to audiences unknown to the writer at the time the speeches were prepared.

Speech Topics

Speech writers do not write only major addresses dealing with critical issues. Writers have the equivalent of what the White House calls "Rose Garden rubbish." Former presidential speech writer John B. McDonald described the types of ceremonial speeches the president is called on to give in the Rose Garden:

Why is the President delighted that Miss Teenage America is calling on him? What does he say to the head of the American Dental Association? What does he tell someone who is off to deliver two musk oxen to the People's Republic of China? What rhetoric is right for the head of an insurance company that has just completed a study of Catholic education? . . . These are real issues and the President can't wing them—somebody has to develop some background and suggestions for lines of credible commentary. (McDonald 1977, A11)

Writers in business as well as government find many occasions— retirement speeches, award presentations, product announcements, and appropriate remarks kicking off a local charity fund drive—to write such talks.

Experience in the Field

Although the speech writing profession has in it some old hands who have had years of experience, the field has many relative beginners. More than half the respondents in the Lichacz study had fewer than five years' experience. Only 2 percent had been writing speeches for twenty years.

Two major explanations can be offered to account for the fact that speech writers do not appear to stay on the job long. One is that there was a boom in speech writing during the 1970s. Many of the speech writing jobs surveyed were new positions, and thus the number of years at the task had to be low. It may be that more and more writers are now becoming career speech writers or at least are staying in the job for longer periods of time than before.

The second explanation can be found in the difficulty of the speech writing task. Heavy demands are placed on writers, and many of them begin to ask to be transferred to a different type of job. Although some writers thrive on the challenges offered by speech writing, others harbor some negative feelings, at least some of the time, toward their work.

OCCUPATIONAL HAZARDS

Because it offers the insights of an experienced writer, an anonymous speech writer's lament is presented below in its entirety:

I have been a speech writer for top executives of a large corporation for nearly twenty years now. In my early days I was enthralled by my work, stimulated by the challenges it presented, and still naive enough to feel complimented when I was asked to write a speech for the president of my company.

But all that has changed. Today, while battling the obligatory midlife crisis and lamenting my misspent youth, I view my work in a vastly different fashion. Far from being enthralled with it, I am painfully bored by it. Instead of a challenge, it is more often a chore. And I don't feel complimented at all. What I really feel like is a bag man—not all of the time, but certainly a large part of the time and most often when I am beginning a new speech.

But I think I am not unusual in my attitude toward my work. Probably most speech writers feel this way from time to time. Those who feel most negatively about their work are those who have been exposed for the longest period of time to five occupational hazards of the job. There may be more than five, but of these I speak with experience and passion.

Anonymity

From the beginning, the unwritten rule in speech writing has been that the writer must remain anonymous. Most of us honor that tradition. Although we may admit to some of our closest friends that we authored this or that speech, to most others who ask, we manage a Mona Lisa smile and say that we merely did some research for the speaker. When the speech hasn't gone over well, of course, we don't mind disclaiming it, and we do so with perhaps more force than necessary. But when a speech has brought the audience to its feet in rousing ovation, that's when it is hardest not to claim some credit for it. Then the writer wants to say, "You're mighty right I wrote that speech. Didn't that analogy knock you out! Wasn't that illustration right on target! How about those smooth transitions! And what a conclusion!" That's what we would like to say, but instead we restrain ourselves and simply join in the applause, reflecting momentarily perhaps on the unfairness of it all.

But I need to distinguish here between anonymity and appreciation. No speech writer expects the audience to cry 'Author, Author' at the conclusion of a speech. Nor does he expect, as Edwin Newman has suggested, that the speaker either open or conclude with the statement, 'This speech was based on an idea by . . .'

Most of us do not want or need public acclaim. What we do want is appreciation for the work we do, especially from the speaker for whom we do it. That appreciation often is not fortcoming. We also want to be able to acknowledge, at least within our company or firm, the kind of work we do. We are not Watergate Plumbers, after all; our work is not something to be ashamed of. And it is demoralizing to spend one's entire career being nonspecific and hedging about one's job. It is also depersonalizing, dehumanizing, and all those other things which whittle away at self-confidence and make it all that much harder to write good speeches. Anonymity is definitely an occupational hazard of the speech writer.

Isolation

The old saying that "Writing is a lonely job" is true. But I think speech writing is the loneliest of all. Other kinds of writers can enjoy the camaraderie of their colleagues, but we speech writers usually don't even know who our colleagues are.

Now I realize that we are not so specialized that we cannot speak to and be understood by other writers or PR personnel. But somehow it's just not quite the same as sharing the problems and frustrations of the job with another of your own kind.

But professional isolation is not the only problem; physical isolation is a problem for the speech writer as well. This may be a problem peculiar only to my own personality, but it is one I have to guard against most carefully. When I am writing a speech, I am totally immersed in it. 'Enmeshed' may be a better word. At any rate, I am preoccupied to the extent that I become antisocial. The longer I wrestle with the problem of how to construct the speech, the more I cut myself off from contact with other people and the more depressed I become. The deeper the depression, the harder it is to work, and so the cycle goes. This is a problem for the speech writer I think because as any psychiatrist will tell you, if you want to demoralize and depress someone, one way to do that is to isolate them. Hence the fear of ostracism in our society or of solitary confinement in prisons. Isolation can be an energy-sapping hazard to the speech writer. The remedy, I've found, is to break the cycle at any point and just go talk with someone.

Staying Too Long in the Job

The problem here is obvious. For the first several months or even years in the speech writing job, you bring a fresh approach to your topics. You haven't yet used up all your jokes or illustrations. You haven't learned what you can't do because of certain policies or regulations. And you haven't had to write on the same topics so often that you can no longer think of anything new to say about them. But after a time, you exhaust your reserves and become a burnt-out case. For me that happened after about five years on the same job writing for the same speaker.

The trick in speech writing is not to write one speech or two speeches. Just about anybody can do that. The real trick is to write the third, fourth, fifth, and sixth speech all on the same topic and to make them interesting. That's tough, because you quickly reach the point where you spend more time desperately wondering what else you can possibly say on the subject than you do in actually saying it. And for me at least, it's almost impossible to write a good speech in a mood of desperation.

Sometimes, however, it isn't necessary to actually leave the job or to change jobs. A short stint at a different kind of writing, or writing for a different speaker may help restore your fine cutting edge. But I'm afraid nothing will help your creativity for writing United Way or Savings Bond speeches year after year. If that's your lot, just tell yourself that's what you get paid for and go ahead and do it. You may also console yourself with the thought that nobody will know whether your speech this year is too much like last year's. They don't remember last year's speech and they won't remember this year's either.

The Demand Nature of the Job

As a speech writer for executives, you're in business to provide a service at the demand of your client. Consequently, try though you might, it's difficult to spread your workload evenly. For example, last month I had only two speeches due this month. It looked like a pretty easy schedule and I even thought about taking a few days off. But in just two days' time, my client accepted four additional speaking engagements, all in one week. So instead of an easy month with vacation time, I've worked right down to the wire, at night and through the weekends. That's to be expected occasionally, but after a time you become exhausted and that's when it becomes a hazard. Any writer needs some down time—time to read, time to clean out files, time to let the mind lie fallow. If you don't have that time, the quality of your work will suffer and so will you. You'll also come to hate your job.

Having to Write on Subjects You Couldn't Care Less About

I've saved this hazard for last because I think it's the most lethal of all. To me there are few things more exhausting than having to reach down within myself and generate enthusiasm for something that inherently bores me stiff. But that is often the lot of the speech writer. Your topics are dictated not by you but by your speaker. You rarely get to write on what you know most about or enjoy most, and it's hard to write an interesting talk on a subject you don't find interesting. Imagine having to write talk after talk on the Salt II agreements, for example, or on the social responsibility of business, or on why you should buy U.S. savings bonds. If you're interested in those topics, fine. But if you're as saturated with them as I am, the only thing worse would be to have to write the "Don't Squeeze the Charmin" commercials. Nothing could be worse than that.

Assignments like those have done more to wear me down to a nub than any of the other hazards I've mentioned altogether. But let's face it: this is not something we can do much about. Such is the essence of our craft, our reason for being on the payroll. Given enough time for research and thought, we are supposed to be able to write interestingly on any subject and to present the best case for our client that we possibly can. That is the responsibility of the advocate and that is our job.

If there is anything we can do to help ourselves and guard against the hazards of being a professional speech writer, it is to recognize our limitations and refuse to take ourselves too seriously. No one can write one outstanding speech after another, especially when you're isolated and anonymous, when you're burned out and bored, or when you have to create an artificial enthusiasm for your topic. All those things just make you a bona fide speech writer. Besides, if you turn out a lousy speech now and then, who knows, you may get out of this crummy job.

These reflections focus mainly on the most negative aspects of speech writing. Certainly most writers encounter some of the problems cited at least occasionally; however, hardly any writer feels completely negative all the time. The lament I have presented was written ten years ago, and the man who wrote it still works in the same industry as a full-time—and highly regarded—speech writer.

CAREER PLANNING

Many professional communicators consider speech writing an excellent career, and others regard it as a likely ladder to a management position.

In attempting to answer the question, "Is there life after manuscript?" Wesley Poriotis has identified some of the factors favoring advancement in management for the speech writer. Drawing on his experience as a management consultant who finds positions for speech writers in top corporations, Poriotis noted the following advantages speech writers possess: involvement in policy formation, experience in clear and analytical thinking, negotiating skills learned in working with speakers and others who must be contacted in the preparation of a speech, and extensive knowledge of the company acquired in writing speeches (Poriotis 1981, 22-23).

There are some disadvantages. Some writers think of their work in narrow, technical terms. They regard themselves as wordsmiths hired to hammer out the language for someone else's ideas, and they fail to assert themselves in finding opportunities to help shape communication strategy. Such writers are especially likely to become isolated from the rest of their organization, and they do not take advantage of the opportunities offered by their position to build useful contacts.

One ironic disadvantage for the speech writer seeking advancement grows out of the shortage of qualified writers. A speaker may be reluctant to see a writer move into management because of the difficulty of finding a replacement. As one speech writer remarked wryly, "My boss says I can't quit; I'm too good!"

The Market

Although speech writing can be a means for advancing to a management post, it is also a rewarding career in itself. In the past, the salary policies of many organizations have been a serious obstacle to speech writing careers. When promotion and salary are based to a significant degree on the number of subordinates a person has, speech writers do not always look good on the organizational chart. Emphasis, however, appears to be shifting from a purely managerial criterion for reward to what we might call a talent criterion.

In weighing an individual's worth, a comparison has often been made between the talent supplied by communications experts in business or government and the talent supplied by actors, singers, and sports figures. Increasingly organizations are willing to recognize that a specialized skill deserves financial reward even though the person with the skill may not supervise a large number of employees.

Leading the way in establishing higher salary levels are the writers for top corporate executives. As a rule, these companies pay more for speech writers than for other communication personnel with comparable years of service. In a 1985 listing of jobs available from Wesley Poriotis's firm, Wesley Brown & Bartle, several positions were available in the $50,000 to $90,000 range with Fortune 500 companies in chemical, consumer packaged goods, and high-tech industries. In contrast to the speech writing jobs, listings for account supervisors and junior vice-presidents cited salaries from $40,000 to $60,000. In the section listing jobs for business journalists for marketing communications and media relations, the salary range was $30,000 to $50,000. Only one salary that did not mention speech writing reached the $60,000 to $70,000 level.

The positions that demand full-time or nearly full-time speech writing tend to pay the most. But even in jobs that require only part-time speech writing or in which the writing is done in smaller companies or for executives below the top rank, salaries for speech writers are still likely to be higher than those for other communications jobs. On the basis of survey data, Lichacz estimated that speech writers were paid $3,000 per year more than the average in the public relations field. James Busse, gathering his information primarily from interviews, concluded that speech writers ranked with those at the top of the salary scale in public relations (Busse 1978, 60). The strong demand for speech writers can be expected to keep pressure on the market to hold speech writing salaries at a high level.

Changing Jobs

One reflection of the prevailing market conditions is the number of management consultants, such as Wesley Poriotis, who specialize in placing speech writers. Jean Cardwell in Chicago and Bill Cantor and Larry Marshall in New York report more openings for speech writers than writers to fill the openings. (The names and addresses of these recruiters appear in the appendix of this book.)

Speech writers will find it advisable to keep up to date on the employment picture. A corporate merger, the transfer of a boss to a new company, or any number of other unforeseen circumstances may dictate a job change. Because speech writers have no specialized professional association and no regular meetings and conferences to attend with their peers, special effort may be required to stay informed. Membership in such organizations as the Public Relations Society of America, the International Association of Business Communicators, and the National Association for Corporate Speaker Activities will keep writers in touch with some of their colleagues and will often provide valuable information about professional opportunities.

Individual writers can do much to prepare for a move should it be required. They should retain at least a few samples of their work; occasionally successive drafts would prove interesting in a private personnel file. A complete list of speeches produced should be kept so they can be summarized by audience and type for a resume. Congratulatory letters and memos should not be discarded, and news clippings might prove valuable. If records are not maintained, the hazard of anonymity that plagues a writer's work can also be a barrier to establishing credentials for a new position.

THE SPEECH WRITING PERSONALITY

A few years ago an effort was made to describe the authoritarian personality. The effort was later largely discredited. The same results await anyone who might attempt to describe the personality traits possessed by speech writers. They fit no pattern. Some are talkative, but others, as one company communications director tactfully put it, are "not highly verbal" in a nonprofessional situation. As a group, they are tidy and unkempt, serious and flippant, casual and formal, and eager and cautious. A few keep their desk tops clean. Many will quickly and somewhat sarcastically reject the suggestion that they "must love words." Most find they think more clearly and work more efficiently with a deadline staring them in the face. But there is no such thing as a speech writer's personality.

The abilities needed by a speech writer are another matter. An ear for the sound of language distinguishes all truly good speech writers. So does a capacity for synthesis, the crucial capacity to draw material from disparate sources to produce a coherent talk. Willingness to work long and uncertain hours is a must. Getting along with people who are in too big a hurry to give out needed information helps. Knowing how to see things from the speaker's perspective (how to become a clone, according to an oil company speech writer) comes easily to most good speech writers.

Speech writers also must have the capacity to cope with intrigue and excitement, especially if they lead lives anything at all like those who have been made the heroes of two modern novels. In *Full Disclosure* (Safire 1977) William Safire casts a young, ambitious speech writer in a leading role in a book advertised as a "sizzling novel of the White House inner circle—where sex and politics are the most natural of allies." In *The Chronicles of Doodah* (Walker 1985), George Lee Walker, a speech writer with experience in the White House and with such companies as Ford and Chrysler, uses a speech writer as narrator in a bizarre satire of life in corporate communications.

Real or fictional, it is hard to characterize the speech writer. But for a highly revealing clue, watch one in the act of writing; they tend to move their lips.

2

Building a Productive
Speaker-Writer Relationship

> The relationship between speechwriter and speechmaker is, by nature,
> fragile and highly personal. It depends on mutual respect and sensitiv-
> ity, and usually takes a period of time to develop fully.
>
> —Burson-Marsteller (1980, 30)

A good working environment can increase efficiency in almost any job, but
nowhere do working conditions affect the quality of the product more than
in speech writing. The actual writing of a speech may be a lonely act, but the
cooperation and understanding of many people, especially the speaker, will
usually be required if the speech is to be a success. Writers need to
acknowledge the special conditions that surround their work, and they must
determine how hard they are willing to press in order to build or maintain
creative, productive working relationships. Three matters demand
attention: direct speaker contact, adequate writing time, and access to
information.

CONTACT WITH THE SPEAKER

Countless speeches have been failures because the speakers did not find
time to work with their speech writers. And a great deal of extra labor has
gone into the revision process in cases where a writer's first communication
from the speaker, coming after the completion of a first draft, was, "This is
not what I had in mind." As Burson-Marsteller points out, a good speech

must accurately reflect the speaker's individuality by giving his personal reaction to a
problem or an issue. . . . This means the chief executive must collaborate with his

public affairs department or his speech writer. All too often the chief executive expects a speech to appear magically on his desk without any contribution on his part. (Burson-Marsteller 1975, 2)

John Bonee speaks of this problem with passion:

If you're in a big organization, any kind of hierarchy, where management is levelized (I don't care if it's business or the church or the academic community) you're going to have people who get between you and the person you're writing for. They are a disruptive force.

You must absolutely insist on seeing your client face-to-face, on interviewing your speaker for every speech. And (if you're writing for the same person regularly) you must have continuous face-to-face contact to get to know that person. Otherwise, you'll be writing just another standard speech. Or you'll be writing for the people between you and the boss instead of for the boss. And that's no good. (Bonee 1982, 201)

Every speech writer needs to have the ability of a Ted Sorensen to be an alter ego for a speaker, to know instinctively how the speaker feels and thinks. But Sorensen had access to John F. Kennedy, and it is that direct access that allows a writer to develop the required insights into a speaker's psyche.

The Initial Conference

A conference should be held between speaker and writer as soon as possible after a speaking engagement has been accepted. A writer may come in with ideas for the speech and even with a tentative outline, but the major purpose of the conference should be to determine what the speaker wants to talk about and what goals the speaker hopes the speech will achieve. Even the speaker who claims to have no ideas for the content of the speech will have a chance to approve or disapprove of the writer's ideas before a lot of time is wasted.

Writers need a high degree of skill in interpersonal communication to hold a satisfactory conference. Because the speaker is an important person whose time is valuable, the writer may be too quick to accept a statement from the speaker without fully understanding it. Especially in the initial meeting, the writer must not be timid in clarifying the speaker's meaning. This may call for a number of statements of the let's-see-if-I've-got-this-straight sort. The writer must sense when to press the speaker for more information and when to accept a vague response as an indication that the writer has leeway to decide a particular issue for the speaker. The writer should listen for words and phrases that may be worked into the speech and should emerge from the meeting with a good set of legible notes. Tape recording the session may be a good idea if it does not bother the speaker.

Care should be exercised in seeing that the wrong people do not get invited to the meeting. Most of the time a two-person conference between speaker and writer is best. Deciding who should attend depends to a great degree on the personalities of the people involved, but a writer's supervisor or manager—especially if that person is not a skilled speech writer—can be a distracting influence. As a general rule, the fewer people who are present, the better the conference is likely to go.

Writers should vigorously resist any efforts of an intermediary to represent the speaker's views as a substitute for a conference. Even if the speaker is reported to be uninterested in the direction of the speech, the addition of an extra person in the communication channel often leads to problems. The intervention of an administrative assistant, for example, may result in an inaccurate account of the speaker's feelings. Even if the intermediary reports the speaker's views correctly, the writer has no opportunity to ask direct follow-up questions. And the writer will be denied the opportunity to pick up nonverbal clues that can be observed when sitting across the desk or sitting beside the speaker on an airplane. The speaker's tone of voice and facial expression will sometimes tell more than words can convey.

Moreover, the motives of the typical intermediary are not always pure. Although major executives and government figures need to be protected by gatekeepers, some of these individuals either do not understand the role of the speech writer or, worse, resent the prestige that direct access brings and the power that it implies. One speech writer characterizes this problem as springing from the "territorial imperatives of other managers who perhaps all too well understand the relationship that often develops between a speaker and a speech writer."

A speech writer who accepts an administrative assistant's forceful version of what the boss wants in the speech may find the assistant's conviction and memory fade rapidly when a speech constructed on such advice is rejected by the speaker. The blame will fall on the speech writer and not on the once-confident individual who claimed to represent the speaker's view so accurately.

The speech writer will not benefit from an adversary relationship with a speaker's representative, however. The first rule for dealing with administrative assistants is to go around them diplomatically, and the second rule is to get along with them—and educate them where necessary—for those occasions when there is no other recourse.

It is true that some writers produce excellent speeches with little or no direct speaker contact. In these cases, the speech fits the speaker because the writer is a little bit of a magician or because the writer created a vision of the speaker from previous experience, from old speeches, and from anybody who was willing to give the writer a clue about the speaker. David Woods, for many years a writer for naval officers and civilian defense officials, often drew on his own military experience combined with the facts in a personnel file to write a speech permeated with the personality of a speaker that Woods had not been able to contact for a single conference. For most writers, that is asking too much.

Follow-up Contacts

After an initial conference to set the direction of the speech, the writer should begin to refine the analysis of the audience, to gather data, and to write a draft. An understanding that the writer's telephone calls will be put through to the speaker with dispatch can be helpful in this period. After the speaker has had a chance to read the draft, a second face-to-face conference should be held.

Any changes the speaker wants should be discussed directly with the writer. If extensive rewriting proves necessary, another conference should be held to repeat the process. As soon as it appears that a substantial amount of the speech is acceptable, the speaker should read the speech aloud with the writer present to allow for fine tuning of language. Words or phrases the speaker stumbles over can be changed, and occasionally a passage may be strengthened by adding or cutting a word to improve the rhythm of the speech.

A speaker who reads a speech aloud in a conference will be more conscious of the importance of the sound of language and may be more open to the use of vivid and compelling language. Reading the speech to the writer may even result in improvements suggested by the speaker. To cite one example, a company vice-president rehearsed a speech urging fast food restaurant owners—for solid corporate reasons—to offer customers a choice of meals on a plate in addition to the carry-out style of eating. A line in the speech, which the speaker had approved after a silent reading, said, "Now they eat their meal from a box." In rehearsal, he spontaneously changed the line to read, "Now they have to dig through a box to eat their meal." It was not a landmark contribution to eloquence, but the change resulted in a better speech and a more confident speaker. Few writers work for speakers of the caliber of Franklin D. Roosevelt, who frequently improved drafts of his speeches. One of his most famous changes was the substitution of the word *infamy* to end a line in his Declaration of War speech that came to him from his writers as "a date which will live in history."

In the follow-up conferences, a writer should not too quickly accept abrupt and arbitrary changes in the substance of the speech. A speaker who has read several drafts of a speech may begin to get bored with it and attempt to strike out in new directions. But if the initial conference laid a solid foundation for the speech, the writer should make an effort to return to that foundation. Reference to notes, along with citations of the speaker's original instructions, may be enough to prevent a great deal of hard work from being wasted. Of course, the writer should be alert for genuine improvements, even if they are major. And if the speaker is adamant about capricious changes, the writer can do little other than comply.

A final prespeech conference for at least some major speeches should include a dress rehearsal.

As often as possible, a speech writer should hear the speech delivered and hold a postspeech conference with the speaker. Far too many speech writers get only vague second-hand reports on how their speeches fared in delivery. Hearing the speech as it is presented gives a writer much valuable information. The response of the audience can be compared with the response the writer expected to get, although the contrast may shock the writer. Humor that sounded fine in the office may fail badly (or a light quip may get a much better reaction than expected). A passage in the talk may get enough overt positive reaction to suggest it could be worked into other speeches.

A tape recording of the speech as delivered may give some of the clues the writer needs and is better than nothing at all. But as General Motors speech writer W. M. Lovell points out, "The only half-way reliable method for discovering individual quirks is to listen while the person makes the speech. The only completely reliable way is to hear that person make several speeches" (Lovell 1978, 12).

A talk with the speaker on the day following the speech or on the way home after the presentation gives the writer a chance to make suggestions on delivery and to determine the speaker's satisfaction with the talk. Especially in the case of a relaxed conversation, many opportunities may arise to build a stronger speaker-writer relationship.

Working with the Speaker: A Case History

Are the above suggestions realistic? Are they practiced by successful writers and speakers? Only sometimes. But when a speaker thinks a speaking opportunity is of great importance, considerable interaction may occur between the speaker and the writer. The following case history illustrates such an instance. The speaker, Florida governor Reubin Askew, had been tapped to give the Keynote Address at the 1972 Democratic National Convention. Sara Newell and Tom King traced the history of the writing of the speech (Newell and King 1972, 346-58).

The speech was written by the governor's speech writer, Roland Page, with the aid of the governor's press secretary and senior executive assistant. After Page got the assignment, his initial conference consisted of lengthy discussions with Askew as Page accompanied the governor on an extended business trip. Even with such close contact with the governor, Page was aware when he submitted the first draft that he had not captured the essence of what his speaker wanted. He was not surprised when, in a follow-up conference with the entire writing staff present, the governor cut out four-fifths of the first effort.

Page then produced a second draft that was discussed at an involved—and unusual—speaker-writer conference. Askew arranged a two-day meeting at a hideaway beach cottage where he and the three writers turned out the third draft of the speech. So intense was their work that when the power failed one night, they continued to work with the aid of a kerosene lantern.

The beach cottage draft became the foundation for the final version of the speech, although nine drafts were finally written. The fourth draft introduced the zingers—the lines designed to evoke applause from convention delegates. The fifth and sixth drafts involved only routine changes in language and structure. As each of these drafts was finished, the governor and his speech writing staff held a conference. They discussed changes, and Askew read each successive draft aloud.

The last three versions of the speech resulted from changes made on the plane and at the convention in Miami Beach. And with all this careful preparation behind him, the governor made sixty-seven minor alterations as he delivered the address.

ADEQUATE WRITING TIME

A speech writer once remarked ruefully, "My boss confuses writing time with typing speed." An important part of a good speaker-writer relationship includes gaining appreciation from the speaker for the complexity of the writing task and the time required to get it done. Some speeches, of course, are easier to write than others, and no precise answer can be given to the question, "How long does it take to write a speech?" Perhaps the best answer in most cases is, "Longer than you think." It is not unusual for a good writer to spend an hour for every minute of delivery time, and that does not count time for research. The hour-per-minute guide deals only with organizing, writing, thinking, and rewriting. It assumes that the facts needed for the speech are on hand, although it does include time for sorting through data and weighing the facts available.

Two Dimensions of Time

In planning a writing schedule for an assignment, writers should recognize two distinct dimensions of time. In addition to the actual writing time, consideration should be given to elapsed writing time—the period between the writing assignment and the final draft. It is one thing to write a speech in a fourteen-hour blitz from ten o'clock Sunday morning until midnight and quite another to distribute the work throughout a normal work week in blocks of time ranging from one to four hours in length.

A speech may be written in an uninterrupted period; that sometimes is the best way. But not always. Frequently writers benefit from the opportunity to move to another task and return to the speech refreshed. A walk in the park or an hour of browsing in the public library may be legitimate alternative activities that will aid in producing better speeches. Even when a speech is written at one sitting, elapsed time is still important in supplying a gestation period before the fingers hit the keyboard. The situations that really hurt are the ones where the speech is due Thursday and the assignment comes in on Tuesday.

Speech writing is a creative activity, and we do not yet fully understand how the human brain functions with such activities. Some research suggests a fuller appreciation of the separate capacities of the brain's hemispheres will help writers work more efficiently. Some writers believe if writing is going very badly, the wrong hemisphere is in temporary control, and they should shift for a time to some more mundane task.

Writer's Block

When writer's block strikes, it may not be possible to put the speech aside for a break that allows a change of pace. Sometimes the job simply has to be done, and writers over the years have developed many stratagems to combat this problem. Some find that dictating instead of keyboarding the words will break the logjam. Others insist that a time and place be set aside for writing, and they force themselves to write no matter how trite or even nonsensical the initial material proves to be.

One useful suggestion is to treat the speech writing task as incremental. The writer can divide a speech writing job into parts, perhaps even going so far as to maintain separate file folders for each part. If the block comes in writing the opening, the writer can go on to work on the first point or the conclusion. When the writing is going well but the speech needs a statistic or a quotation, a blank space can be left on the page and the writing continued. The trick is to avoid letting a barrier for any one part of the speech become a barrier for the speech as a whole.

No incentive to completing a speech compares with the motivation supplied by a deadline. The adrenaline flows, the words come, and somehow the speech that could not be written yesterday can be written today.

The magical power of the deadline cannot be denied, but no one should conclude that it is unnecessary to plan for adequate writing time spread over a reasonable period of days or weeks. If sufficient time has been set aside to write the speech, the writer has the luxury of using the incentive supplied by a deadline to make a few incisive revisions in the manuscript. Even when the well-planned speech is completed in a flurry of activity minutes before the boss is scheduled to get it, that speech will quite likely have benefited from the incubation time and reflection time allowed by having a good writing schedule.

Adequate Writing Time: A Case History

A power company in the northwestern United States has developed a sound procedure for allowing enough time to write speeches. The system it uses is set forth in the following memo. The names of individuals have been omitted, but the text of the memo has not otherwise been changed:

TO: Manager, Communications
FROM: Speech Writer
SUBJECT: Preparation of Speeches

In order to have a speech in final form 10 days in advance of its presentation, it is necessary that:

1. I be notified of the date the speech is to be given about six weeks in advance.
2. Sufficient work time be allocated exclusively for preparation of the speech.

An ideal typical schedule would be as follows:

1. Notification of date of speech	
2. Researching the location, audience, local facts	(2-3 days)
3. Contact program chair to determine topic	(1-2 days)
4. Confer with the speaker to determine how the topic should be approached and to determine whether slides or other visuals should be used	
5. Research topic—select slides	(5 days)
6. Prepare speech	(5 days)
7. Review by speaker and others affected	(5 days)
8. Corrections or rewrite	(1 day)
9. Final review by speaker	(2-3 days)
10. Final preparation and typing	(1 day)

While the total time involver is 22 to 25 working days, the speech would be on the speaker's desk for preliminary review 10 days before it is to be given.

This schedule does not mean that speeches must be scheduled six weeks apart. It means primarily that I must know that far ahead of time so that the work can proceed in an orderly fashion. More than one could be done at the same time and with the development of a good, basic speech, the research and preparation time could be shortened.

Each speech is tailored to a specific audience. In speaking to groups such as Chambers of Commerce, Kiwanis, Rotary or other service clubs, the speaker's credibility is enhanced if he knows some facts about the geographic area, or the town, and can make some local references. This involves contacting persons in the club, or the local utility to obtain the information.

It is also necessary to obtain information on the meeting itself, i.e., the date, time, length of time allowed for the speech, the size and composition of the audience, the meeting place and the master of ceremonies.

The amount of time required for research depends upon the topic. If it is a simple "Company Story" type of speech, research time is minimal.

If it is a more technical speech, assistance may be needed from the technical staff and extra time must be allowed.

To determine a topic, it is necessary, in many cases, to confer with the program chair to determine the wishes of the audience.

It is vital that I confer with the speaker to discuss the topic and the manner in which it is to be approached, as well as whether there will be visual aids.

Writing of the speech takes a minimum of one week. Another week should be allowed for review by others to assure accuracy of figures or statements. This has not always been done, but it is recommended.

Time must be allowed for rewriting or corrections, final review and final typing.

It would be a service if the speech could be reproduced to use as a handout for the media reporters. And, if there is sufficient time, a news release could be prepared for distribution on the day of the speech.

The critical factors involved in having a speech prepared 10 days in advance are that there is sufficient advance notice and that sufficient time can be allocated exclusively for work on the speech.

Without this, the schedule fails.

ACCESS TO INFORMATION

Staffing the speech, the process of submitting the speech to appropriate key people for their reaction and help, can easily upset the delicate speaker-writer relationship. While staffing can be invaluable in uncovering new ideas, checking for accuracy of data, and making sure that no policy violations have worked their way into the speech, the writer runs the danger of losing control of the speech. Although editors and other public relations and communications people must contend with the approval process, speeches more than any other form of communication seem to awaken the desire to meddle with a writer's work. A writer may suddenly find many people vying for the mind and heart of the speaker, and the speech can suffer as a result.

The Manuscript Route

The speech writer should fight to uphold one cardinal principle: no one must be allowed to tamper with the manuscript as it travels from writer to speaker and back again. No one should change the writer's work and send it directly to the speaker. Changes made by the speaker should go directly to the writer ideally in a face-to-face meeting.

Copies of a preliminary draft of the speech, or perhaps copies of only a section of the speech, may travel to the desk of an engineer, an accountant, a vice-president, or a lawyer. But the manuscript, with any suggested changes, should return directly to the speech writer. Even the writer's editor or supervisor, who may insist on seeing and altering the manuscript before it goes forward, should make no unilateral changes.

John Bonee describes how the system should work:

When I got a new boss recently, I said to him, "Look, I don't know how you're used to operating, but I'll tell you how I like to operate. When I give you a manuscript, you don't have to send it to the law department, you don't have to send it to our rates and revenue people, you don't have to send it to the marketing types. If I'm doing my job, I've been there. I've talked to them. I've let them review the first draft long before I gave it to you. If anything is wrong, I take the responsibility." (Bonee 1982, 201)

Word Molesters

Even the best-organized system will not protect the writer from the urge of advisers to meddle gratuitously with the language of a speech. Handling these word molesters calls for confidence and courage on the part of a writer. Technical experts are likely offenders. They sometimes value the preciseness of their jargon over the goal of being understood by an audience. Financial experts often have a language of their own, and even the occasional amateur grammarian may insist on correctness when a split infinitive might be the better way to subtly slip a point into a speech.

Many lawyers have been highly successful speech writers, but in their purely legal role in organizations, they are at times a force for extreme caution and even timidity in speeches. And they occasionally write in a language only remotely similar to English. Concern with the influence of lawyers produced one bit of speech writing verse:

> There once was a speech writer in Hell
> Who wrote for the devil so well
>> He got a raise in his pay
>> To an ice cube a day
> And the lawyer was removed from his cell

When changes are suggested in parts of the speech unrelated to an adviser's area of competence, the writer can rather easily ignore the suggestions. When proposed changes cause problems in the speech but at the same time involve scientific or legal matters with which the writer is not familiar, some effort at compromise may be in order. At the very least, a properly structured communications office will not allow the staffing process to result in changes made without the writer's knowledge. The writer then has a chance to make an argument for expressing the proposed ideas not in jargon but in lucid prose.

A White House Example

President Jimmy Carter, with a methodical approach to the problem, had a well-organized White House speech writing staff. Although at one point Carter's chief speech writer resigned with some pointed criticism of the President (Fallows 1979, 33-35), the process used by his writers was sound. The account presented here is based on an interview conducted in the spring of 1980 with Carter's deputy chief speech writer, Gordon Stewart. According to Stewart, when a speech writing assignment came to the staff, a single writer was picked to handle it. The writer then prepared a draft of the speech, which was labeled B-1. This draft was circulated to appropriate advisers, such as cabinet officers, who had an interest in the area under consideration.

If it proved necessary to send a second draft back to any or all of the advisers, that draft was labeled B-2. It would typically incorporate some suggestions and reject others. Some differences were worked out informally, but if a ranking Carter adviser insisted on having an alternative to the writer's version presented to the president, that alternative would be included in the A-1 draft—the first draft to reach the President—essentially in the form of a footnote. Thus the President could easily make the final decision. Mr. Carter, Stewart said, "wanted the infighting done" before he saw the speech.

Subsequent drafts to the President were identified as A-2, A-3, and so on until a final draft won approval. Stewart noted that under President Carter, a few drafts were usually sufficient.

Positive Features of the Staffing Process

The approval process on balance has more advantages than disadvantages if writer uses it well. The quality of suggestions and corrections can be improved, for example, if the writer cultivates a network of experts and advisers from whom help might someday be expected.

Building relationships with potential contributors before they are actually needed is better than approaching them cold when their help may be needed quickly. The writer who gets to know advisers on a personal level ahead of time will probably get better results than one who telephones a stranger at the last minute. Building rapport also makes it easier to use staff people for more than just facts; they can often supply anecdotes about the speaker or the company, and they may have ideas or suggestions that help the speaker far beyond the immediate needs of a single speech.

Anyone who helps in the writing of the speech should get some feedback from the writer. If someone in research and development supplies data for a speech, that person should get some indication from the writer that the help was useful in the final speech. Sending a memo with a copy of the speech attached may ensure that assistance will be available the next time it is called for.

Writers at times encounter a reluctance on the part of some to divulge information. After all, knowledge is power, and few people want to surrender what they may regard as highly confidential facts about plans for a new product or the expected impact of a management decision. The writer has to learn to say, "I am helping the president put together some material for a speech" in such a tone that the holder of the information gets the clear impression that the writer is the true agent of the speaker. The process of gathering data requires a blend of charm and assertiveness.

THE ASSERTIVE WRITER

In all aspects of their work, from seeking direct contact with speakers to getting adequate time to do their work to improving the staffing process, writers must determine how forward they wish to be in attempting to affect their working conditions. Because so few people understand the speech writing process, little is likely to be done to improve it if the writer does not speak out. The question then becomes how assertive the writer should be.

Some writers have made their peace with their jobs and have given up trying to establish a productive work environment. They work with little or no speaker contact, write speeches hastily when adequate notice could have been given, and settle for a minimum of solid material to include in their speeches. Other writers boldly insist on a good working relationship as a condition for staying on the job. If they cannot improve conditions, they quit. Some leave quietly. Some, like Robert Shrum in departing the campaign of Jimmy Carter, go out with a blast (Shrum 1976, 34-40).

Most writers fall somewhere in the middle. They do not passively accept their fate, but neither do they make demands that threaten their job security. Such writers simply look for all opportunities to push for changes. In some cases, speakers have never been asked, or have not been asked often enough, for more conferences with their writers. It may be the writer's supervisor who is reluctant to make the request or does not understand its importance. In the case of getting inadequate notice of speaking engagements, it may be that no one has bothered to ask the speaker's secretary if carbons of letters of acceptance can be forwarded to the writer. Or perhaps it has simply never occurred to anyone that the speech writer should attend meetings where important issues are being decided, meetings that would give the writer useful facts as well as provide on opportunity to learn background and observe the speaker talking off the cuff.

In any one of these situations, a gentle push from the writer may get results—if not the first time, then maybe the second or the third time. Writers need to look for opportunities to improve their situations. Staff meetings or performance reviews may provide an opening for a frank discussion of needed changes. Writers can set forth their needs in a memo or position papers to get the issues out in the open.

Where possible, managers and supervisors should be made into allies by getting them involved in the common goal of improving the speech writer's product. Where managers are disinterested, the ingenuity of the speech writer should come into play. A writer new on the job is especially well positioned to be slow to learn the old rules that limit the effectiveness of the writing task.

In some cases, a consultant may be brought in to examine the speech writing process. Such a service is a variation of the communication audit many organizations use routinely. The outside consultant's opinion may contain nothing the people inside the organization do not already know, but it often has more weight than opinion coming from within.

THE SPEECH WRITER AS POLICY MAKER

A successful relationship with a speaker depends in part on the writer's full understanding that speech writing is more than dressing up someone else's ideas. Chrysler speech writer Charles Connolley observed,

In my case, when my client is Mr. Iacocca, I have to become a surrogate chairman. When I have to write the top man's speech, I'm literally forced to figure out policy, compress it, and make it cogent from the point of view of the Chairman. Therefore, when I sit in on meetings to dig for my information, I'm not just a recorder, I'm a strategist. (Poriotis 1981, 22)

A top writer at another major company said, "Often top management does not create policy at all in a formal sense. . . . Management may have only vague ideas on a subject. These ideas will often be clarified, stated and established in policy form only through a business speech" (Poriotis 1981, 22).

Speech writers, then, do not act as mere parrots. They often find themselves deeply involved in decision making. Any writer who works for an official who speaks in public for an organization may help form policy. This comes about in three ways: phrasing policy, forcing policy, and formulating policy.

Phrasing Policy

A writer may phrase policy. The speech writer functions in this role as articulator. A company or agency policy may never have been committed to paper. When the writing process begins, the nuances of language suddenly take on great importance. The writer must put into print that which has been previously communicated only orally. Drafts of such a speech may produce long arguments over a word or a clause. Eventually the writer must sit down and hammer out a speech that puts the organization on record.

Many corporations recognize that speeches become a printed record of company policy. General Electric publishes executive speeches in a format that permits ready filing and easy retrieval. The speeches are distributed with catalog code numbers on the back page, and they have punched holes in the margin to permit them to be bound for handy reference.

Forcing Policy

At some point in the process of speech preparation, a writer may shift from the role of articulator of policy and become the catalyst who forces a policy into being. The writer may simply be unable to complete a passage on government regulation or environmental safeguards without a determination of the company's official position.

Speeches in politics and government are more likely to create or force a policy than are speeches in business, or at any rate examples are easier to find in government. Harry Truman once articulated a major foreign policy position primarily because he needed to make a speech. Jimmy Carter's writers wrote a speech for a farm audience and discovered they had to ask for a change in Department of Energy policies to avoid conflict between what the President was going to say and established government procedure. And just as President Nixon did not have an official position on the social significance of Miss Teenage America before she appeared in the Rose Garden, the president of Ajax Widgets may not have a position on company support for tax reform until called on to deliver a speech on the subject.

Formulating Policy

Documented cases of speech writers' actively playing the role of policy maker are easier to find in politics than in business writing. This may be because political writers are more aggressive in their demands, or it may be that political writers are less modest in their claims. Whatever the explanation, political writers are often quite open about discussing their influence on their speakers. Speech writer Mel Grayson, for instance, boasted that a major shift in federal policy on price controls was "mine, all mine, and mine alone" (Grayson 1978, 65). Grayson said that he put the policy statement in a Houston speech by Vice-President Agnew without any guidance from White House policy advisers, and Grayson speculated that his idea became the basis for other official statements and perhaps even for changes in market prices.

Robert Shrum, one of the speech writers for the widely noted 1981 Democratic Convention speech by Senator Edward F. Kennedy, has written for a number of major politicians, including former Senator Edmund Muskie. In his efforts to get Muskie to come out early in opposition to military aid for Vietnam, Shrum repeatedly wrote into the senator's speeches statements taking that position. Finally worn down by his speech writer, Muskie gave up. As Shrum described it, "It took eight months of putting it in speeches and getting it knocked out, of arguing with him, of slowly turning Clifford and Warnke around by getting them to think it was their idea" (Devlin 1974, 10).

Changing Perceptions

Although corporate writers are generally more guarded in relating the details of their influence, Mel Grayson is no doubt right in correcting the public impression of speech writers as intellectual stenographers. One indication that corporations are recognizing the policy role of speech writers can be found in subtle changes in the language some companies use in the job titles of speech writers.

More and more frequently the word *policy* appears in job titles and department names. W. M. Lovell, for example, was named GM's director of policy coordination, and Frank Stokes of Monsanto was given the title director of policy analysis and communication. Writers of speeches have suffered for years under titles apparently designed in some cases to obscure rather than clarify the role of the writer. "Editorial assistant" and "communication specialist" are not titles likely to help identify speech writers or give them much power or status.

Advertisements for jobs also contain language reflecting an awareness of the speech writer as more than a parrot of someone else's ideas. Recent samples include: "[writer] will be involved with planning and developing themes and messages''; ''accessibility to top management and opportunity to take on the tough issues go along with the job''; and ''help needed in articulating company's social concerns.''

SPECIAL CONSIDERATIONS

A number of special considerations affect the writer's working environment, although they are not strictly part of the speaker-writer relationship.

Writing by Committee

There is merit in Ted Sorensen's contention that ''group authorship is rarely if ever successful'' because ''a certain continuity and precision of style, and unity of argument must be carefully drafted'' (Sorensen 1963, 61). The fact remains, however, that many speeches will involve the hand of more than one writer.

There are actually some advantages to having more than one writer working on a talk. As Joseph Persico, once a speech writer for Nelson Rockefeller, noted, there are occasions when ''speechwriters might visit each other's cubicles and try to strike creative sparks off one another'' (Persico 1972, 59). And Persico commented favorably on the advantages of having a chief speech writer who served as editor and could, based on long experience with the speaker, make changes in a writer's copy to make sure the language fit the Rockefeller style. An editor, as in the case of any other type of writing, may well be the speech writer's best friend. Phillips Petroleum Company is among the corporations that have smoothly functioning writing staffs with excellent relations between editors and speech writers.

Editing is a term that might be applied to much of the work speech writers do. Often a writer starts a speech with a great deal of material written by someone else or by a number of other writers. This material could include financial statements, reports, articles, or even old speeches. The writer's task may be less to create than to combine. In the process, the uniformity of style and argument Sorensen mentioned must be imposed.

In addition to the unseen and perhaps unknown persons who supply the speech writer with raw material for a speech, there will at times be more than one writer at work on a given speech. When this happens, early coordination among writers can be helpful. Lois Einhorn has experimented with various approaches to group writing in her college speech writing classes. In discussing her work, she has found that groups were more successful when they began with a ''prewriting conference'' than when they worked separately and attempted to merge their individual work into a single draft. Joseph Persico found in working with Rockefeller that a "story conference," held soon after a speaking calendar was established, was useful in generating ideas for speeches and in coordinating efforts of the writers.

Free-Lance Writing

Working as a free-lance speech writer creates a special relationship between speaker and writer. In spite of some of its problems, the free-lance approach has great appeal to both writers and speakers.

From the writer's point of view, writing speeches "off duty" may provide needed variety and challenge. As an opportunity to make additional money, it has the advantage of being done privately, and it can fit into odd moments of available time. The freedom and independence of free-lance work lures some writers, after they have established sufficient contacts, into working on their own full time.

The advantages from an organization's perspective are often even more compelling. Since a speaking schedule is sometimes unbalanced, with periods of intense activity followed by slack periods, a free-lance writer can be a welcome addition during the time of overload. Some organizations may find the free-lance approach a permanent solution to their speech writing needs, even if a large number of speeches is needed. Avoiding problems of company infighting is another advantage. When the writer is an outsider on temporary assignment, direct access to a major executive is less likely to ruffle feathers.

Many companies are reducing staff and farming out public relations jobs. The free-lance writer is part of a growing move toward decentralization. The financial arrangements can be advantageous to both parties. A company has less overhead, and the successful writer can expect to be paid at at least the same rate that would be earned in full-time work.

Fees for free-lance speech writing vary considerably. One writer offers prepackaged commencement speeches for about $25. In another case, a public relations firm charged $50,000 for a single speech. In that instance, the company claimed to have lost money because the speech was given in a foreign country with simultaneous translation and was accompanied by a sophisticated multimedia presentation. Obviously most fees fall between these extremes. When research time is added to writing time, $1,500 to $2,500 is not unusual for a fairly typical fifteen- to twenty-minute speech.

Facilities

The ideal speech writer's office is private, with windows providing a relaxing view and equipped with the latest model word processor. Files bulge with choice bits of data the writer has socked away. A research staff is located nearby with a computer that quickly calls up the latest statistics. There is a sofa for a couple of hours sleep when the writer has to work all night.

CONCLUSION

Perhaps no speech writer has a perfect relationship with a speaker or an ideal working environment. In many respects, however, the White House writers come close. When speaking is as important as it is in the case of the president of the United States, a speaker is not likely to expect a speech to appear magically on the desk. Even with a staff of writers to turn out his speeches, Franklin Roosevelt involved himself extensively in their work. As one of his writers reported, FDR's schedule fell one or two days behind when he worked with his writers on a major speech (Rosenman 1952, 12).

In the Ford White House, head speech writer Robert Orben described how the President cooperated with his writers:

President Ford gave an estimated 1200 speeches during his term of office and all were conceived, developed, rewritten, and polished based on his direction and guidance received from meetings in the Oval Office. We usually had two meetings a week with President Ford. One to discuss the concept and content of future speeches. A second to review, page by page, drafts of immediately upcoming speeches. We knew precisely what he liked, what he didn't like, and what he wanted changed. On very important messages, such as the State of the Union, the President might bring in pages of handwritten text to give us the precise wording he wanted on a sensitive point. It was an ideal and very productive relationship. (Orben 1982, 20)

3

Analyzing Audiences and Setting Speech Objectives

Rhetoric finds its end in judgment—for the audience judges the counsels that are given.

—Aristotle, *The Rhetoric*

Speech as a medium of communication has many advantages over other means of expressing an idea. No other medium allows a message to be tailored to fit its receivers so well. No other medium permits such extensive, immediate feedback.

To exploit the strengths of speech communication, a writer must have in mind a clear picture of the audience and a clear notion of how the speech is to affect the audience. A speech may fail badly if it is written on the basis of faulty assumptions about the audience. Consider, for example, a speech prepared without any realization of intense hostility felt by the listeners toward the speaker's cause. Other speaking opportunities are wasted because the intended effect of the speech was not appropriate. A typical example of this failure is the speech that merely aims to inform when a call for action would better serve the speaker's cause.

The analysis of the audience affects the determination of the goal of the speech. While a writer may begin preparing a speech with a goal in mind, that goal must be evaluated in the light of what the writer learns about the audience. Audience analysis may suggest a more modest goal than the writer had hoped for, or it may reveal that the writer's initial expectations were too modest.

AUDIENCE ANALYSIS

Writers often fail to collect more than a few pieces of information about an audience and choose to rely instead on stereotyping. The theory seems to be, "If you've seen one Rotary Club, you've seen'em all." Sometimes this approach works out well, and the speech is a success. Even in these cases, however, a good analysis of the audience might have produced some bits of data that would have helped the writer localize the speech or give it a friendlier tone. The return on the investment of time spent in sizing up the audience may be small, but the writer's time will not be wasted.

Sometimes hasty audience analysis results in a mediocre speech, one that fails to take into account subtle but critical features of a particular audience. The speech may bore the audience or make listeners angry. A thorough audience analysis in such a case would have turned up a set of facts that would have saved the writer from disaster or perhaps even made the speech into a roaring success.

Guidelines

Three useful rules should guide the speech writer in doing a thorough analysis of an audience. First, the writer should not rely on information gathered from just one source. The writer's most obvious contact with the host organization will probably be the person in charge of the program. The program chair and other officers of the organization can supply valuable information, but they tend to give polite or official answers that may lack the depth the writer needs. The principal of a school, for example, will probably give a rosier account of the PTA than a writer would get by also calling on a trusted former teacher. Any personal friend of the writer who belongs to the organization should be asked for help. The speaker's own organization may sponsor memberships in various service clubs, and these people may prove to be useful.

For speeches out of town, contacts in the press might be able to supply needed facts. So will someone who wrote a speech previously given to the group.

A second rule is to get some data orally. The neat, printed forms used by many communication departments to gather audience information can be helpful, but answers tend to be brief and superficial. Even a lengthy written answer does not provide the extra insights available from tone of voice and facial expression. A request for information on educational background may be answered on a form with the words, "Fifty percent have graduate degrees," whereas a conversation over a drink might produce, "Half the group's a bunch of smark-aleck eggheads." Even over the telephone, informers tend to be more informative than they would be in writing.

The third rule calls for the writer to use indirect as well as direct sources of information. Returning to the case of the out-of-town speech, some background reading in local newspapers may produce relevant material. Newsletters, membership fliers, and a variety of other publications can give the writer insight into an organization. Anyone who has to write a college commencement speech should consider browsing through a file of campus newspapers and maybe look at a few back issues of the college annual in order to absorb some local color.

Usefulness of Data

Writers may do a better job of collecting data on an audience if they appreciate the fact that this information is valuable on two levels. First, the data may directly affect the substance of the speech by dictating appropriate material and language for the speech, as well as the choice of a goal of the speech. Second, the data may provide for both writer and speaker a welcome degree of psychological comfort by reducing the fear of the unknown.

Substance. As experienced writers know, the content of a good speech changes slightly as the speaker goes from audience to audience even though the subject of the speech remains constant. A glaring example of the failure to observe this rule can be seen in the case of a speaker who pulled from the files a speech once delivered to an all-male club and gave it word for word to an audience that was more than 50 percent female. Among the speaker's problems was the repeated use of such statements as "as your wives know," "if you ask your wife," and "as your wives will tell you." This is not to suggest that a brand-new speech has to be written for every audience—that is often a great waste of a writer's time—but every speech about to be repeated should be reviewed in the light of specific facts known about the new audience.

Comfort. On a second level, a clear and accurate image of the audience provides a much higher degree of psychological comfort for a writer than would be the case if the audience is little more than a mental blur. One writer struggling with a speech to be delivered to a service club went to one of its meetings as an observer and returned to his office to write a solid speech because he had a clear vision of the target of his message. Most writers will discover that they have great trouble getting the words to flow well if the speech opens with an implicit "To whom it may concern."

The speaker, too, gains psychological comfort from knowing about the audience. Writers should attach to every draft of a speech a cover sheet setting forth relevant facts about the audience. The speaker might even benefit from something as simple as a sketch showing the arrangement of the meeting room and indicating who will be at the head table.

A Checklist for Audience Analysis

After a speech has ended, it is usually easy to look back and see the kinds of audience information that should have been collected to make the talk succeed. Knowing the right questions to ask ahead of time is more difficult. With experience, a writer can develop a checklist that will uncover appropriate information. The items offered here do not by any means include everything that might be required, but they do offer a starting point.

Name of the Group. Be sure to get the group's name exactly right. If the audience is a Jaycee chapter in Gotham City, it may be the West End chapter or it may be the Southside chapter, and the two may have a heated rivalry. The story is perhaps apocryphal, but the writer who prepared a speech for the Handicapped Bowlers League should have written one for the Handicap Bowlers League.

Date and Time. It wouldn't hurt for the writer to be aware of the fact if a speech will be delivered on Halloween or Lincoln's birthday. April Fool's day may not be the best time to write a speech making a new product announcement, and an appropriate reference to St. Patrick's Day may give a speech a fresh topical tone. A breakfast speech does not usually offer a good opportunity for hearty humor, while an evening talk may require special effort to gain and keep the attention of an audience. A speech should be adapted to the time and date, or the time and date should be changed to fit the speech.

Physical Setting. To help ensure the speaker's psychological comfort, a writer may wish to supply the speaker with an advance description of the setting in which the speech will be given. This could include a diagram showing who is at the head table, how the room is arranged, and where the lectern will be located. In a few instances, a historic location may be of enough importance for the speaker to comment on it in the speech, or, in the case of an address to be delivered out of doors, location may affect the content by demanding more dynamic material.

Desired Length of Speech. The modern business speech delivered to the public usually runs about twenty minutes. Political speeches and in-house business speeches tend to last longer. The writer needs to know what length is expected by the audience and what provisions are to be made for including a question-and-answer (Q&A) session in the time allotted. Ten to fifteen minutes for Q&A following a fifteen- to twenty-five-minute speech will be about right for most service club talks. In most situations, writers should attempt to dissuade speakers from agreeing to talk for forty-five minutes or more.

Brevity is not so great a virtue that it calls for giving only a five- or ten-minute public talk unless a meeting runs overtime. The writer should find out the usual adjournment time of a meeting and pass this information on to the speaker. When a meeting does last beyond the time listeners expect to leave, speakers will often find it wise to eliminate the Q&A or even to make drastic cuts in the speech itself. If this eventuality can be anticipated, the writer may be able to mark the manuscript to suggest where material can be best omitted.

Nature of the Program. Because a speech is not given in a vacuum, a writer needs to learn as much as possible about the nature of the program of which the speech will be a part. If the program includes a social hour, the writer needs to know something about the usual mood of the audience after a few drinks. The writer should determine if the speech should refer to some special occasion, such as boss's night or awards' night. Perhaps a business meeting has been put on the agenda to follow the speech, in which case plans should be made to spirit the speaker away to avoid the awkwardness of an unwilling spectator at a dull discussion of the club's budget.

Other Speakers. No writer should assume any one speech will be the only presentation at a meeting and should find out if other speakers will be present. This information will give the writer the opportunity to coordinate the speaker's talk with other remarks and may help avoid an embarrassing situation. A speaker who will be preceded by a moving address on drug addiction might not be able to use the piece of humor the writer found so effective the last time the speech was delivered.

Unusual Events. There should be no surprises. A famous news correspondent once watched what he apparently assumed was to be a serious event grow steadily more giddy. The last straw came shortly before the correspondent's speech when someone dressed in an armadillo costume led the entire group in a rather unusual dance. The speaker was forced to throw away his prepared text and substitute a much more informal presentation.

Knowing in advance about unusual events will help the writer prepare a talk to fit the occasion. Or the writer may be in a position to suggest that offbeat program events be altered or cancelled. For example, a gag gift for the speaker that is intended in a spirit of wholesome fun could ruin a speech if it is not known about and properly coordinated with the speech.

Audience Size. Although the size of the audience ordinarily has little effect on the subject matter of a speech, it can have an effect on such features as the degree of formality of the language of the talk. Also, a speaker's morale may drop considerably if the speaker expects a huge crowd, but only a handful of listeners appear. The reverse is also true; the speaker will be protected from shock if warned in advance by the writer that the crowd will be much larger than the speaker usually addresses.

Gender. In most speeches, the ratio of men to women will make little difference. But in some cases a heavy preponderance of one sex or the other, taken in combination with other facts gathered, may cause a writer to support a point with different illustrations or statistics than otherwise would have been used. For example, an audience made up of 90 percent women could be expected to appreciate more readily the implications of an illustration of a balance of trade problem if it is based on imported shoes rather than imported ball bearings. The rule would not necessarily hold if the women were mechanical engineers. Nor would the ball bearing illustration be necessarily wise for an audience of male shoe clerks.

Even if the information about sex makeup of the audience does not affect the content of the speech, it would be an example of useful information for the psychological comfort of the speaker and the writer. The clearer the image of the audience, the better job both speaker and writer are likely to do.

Ethnic Groups. Many corporations recruit for their speakers' bureaus employees who speak the native language of ethnic groups among the customers of the companies. While adaptation of a speech to fit an audience does not often call for the use of a language other than English, other more subtle adaptations may be in order.

Again remembering that other factors need to be considered in conjunction with ethnic makeup of an audience, the fact that a significant percentage of Mexican-Americans or French-Canadians will be present can alter the substance of a speech. The American Heart Association has used an audience analysis form for speaker bureau members that calls for a check into ethnic backgrounds of audiences. If it is discovered that blacks will be in attendance, speakers are instructed to include relevant material on high blood pressure supplied by the association.

Age. Older citizens have been active in recent years in organizing to protect their interests. This movement demonstrates the importance of reaching older listeners and suggests a level of special concerns that writers must examine. Younger audiences also have special interests, and messages must be shaped to fit a group that will often have considerable buying power, as well as minds not fully made up on some crucial issues.

Any writer who has had to produce a commencement address knows how difficult it is to appeal to both parents and their children in a single speech. In an ordinary speech, the failure to find out the age of the audience can lead to a talk that fails to touch the listeners.

Education and Occupation. In a typical case of audience analysis, a sketch of listeners' educational backgrounds and their occupations will provide a writer with valuable clues to aid in making the speech fit the situation. When a speaker intends, for example, to slam the legal profession or take a poke at government service, the need for appropriate care in choice of words will suddenly become apparent if the writer learns that lawyers and civil servants will be in the audience.

Special Persons Present. Because a speech should be a personal form of communication, writers need to know something about not just the audience as a whole but about individuals in the audience as well. An effort should be made to find out if there will be any special persons present that the speaker should know about. A harsh critic of the speaker's position may attend, or a close personal friend of the speaker may be in the audience. The writer can protect a speaker from awkward situations by knowing about such people.

Alf Goodykoontz, executive editor of the *Richmond Times-Dispatch* and a popular speaker, makes a habit of mentioning two or three names of members of his audience during a talk. Speech writers can make effective use of the "Goodykoontz rule" to help a speaker build a bond with the audience. In working the names into the manuscript, it is necessary to take some precautions. If the speaker cannot be depended on to check the matter out before the speech, then the reference must be made in a general way. It's safer to write, "I'm sure Mayor Snort will be happy to learn . . ." than "I'm sure, Mayor Snort, that you will be happy to learn . . ."

Knowledge and Opinion. It is easier to gather demographic data than to play the role of a pollster in order to learn what is inside the minds of listeners. Yet a speech must make some effort to discover an audience's level of knowledge and opinion on the subject of the speech. It may be worth the effort in important speeches to pay for professional help in polling opinion. But for the most part, writers rely on their own interviews and reading to judge the audience's level of knowledge and opinion.

A speech should avoid the extremes. Telling an audience something it knows so well that nothing can be added is as bad as telling an audience something above its ability to grasp. A ringing speech arguing for a point listeners accepted long ago wastes as much time as a powerful effort to change minds that are completely closed on a subject. Only by understanding what an audience knows and thinks can a writer avoid these dangers.

Audience Analysis: A Case History

Few speeches cause more headaches for the writer than the commencement address. An outstanding job of audience analysis made a major contribution to the success of a speech written by Dick Charlton and Kathie Kornack of J I Case for delivery by Morris W. Reid, Case's chairman of the board, before a graduating class at Carthage College.

The writers began their audience analysis by preparing a questionnaire and sending it along with a personal letter from Mr. Reid to every member of the Carthage graduating class. The large number of replies they got gave them an excellent description of the primary audience for the speech. The students supplied data on their education and their job interests. They revealed their attitudes on economics, politics, families, government versus business careers, and the role of women in society. Nearly half of those responding accepted the invitation to make comments to supplement their answers.

The writers used the data in three ways. First, the information from the questionnaire helped shape the intended goal of the address. On the basis of the students' feelings revealed in the survey, Charlton and Kornack wrote a speech designed to reinforce positive attitudes about the country and the economy. Second, they used the replies from the students for much of the content of the speech. Student comments were quoted in the speech, and the entire survey was summarized in the middle of the address. Third, a printed summary of the survey was distributed at the conclusion of the ceremony as a memento of the occasion for the graduates. The summary was included at the end of a copy of the speech. (In the speech, students had been told they would get the results of the survey and were asked to save the questions to ask their own children in twenty-five years.)

As a final touch in adapting the speech to the audience, each student received a quotation taken from the conclusion of the address and encased with a bicentennial silver dollar. Although few occasions will demand or even permit such extensive audience analysis, the principle on which the writers proceeded has universal application: Know your audience.

DETERMINING SPEECH OBJECTIVES

A speech writer was sitting in his office late one afternoon when his boss stopped by. "You know that convention I'm going to next month," the boss said, "well, they want me to give a speech."

The speech writer reached for pen and paper as he asked, "What about?"

The boss gave his answer over his shoulder as he started out of the office and down the hallway. "About twenty minutes," he answered.

The story is factual. Worse, it represents an attitude about giving speeches that is all too common. Many speakers and speech writers regard the primary purpose of a talk as filling an allotted time slot on a program. This is not to say they regard the content as totally unimportant; it's just that they see the aim of the speech as doing little more than honoring a request. Beyond a vague expectation that the speaker and perhaps the speaker's organization will gain a little gratitude, such writers and speakers do not think much about the objectives that a speech might accomplish.

While any speech writer might be required some day to write a throwaway speech, a professional writer should fully appreciate the power of a speech to have an impact on an audience. That impact is measured by the extent to which the audience is moved by the speaker's words, and before every speech the writer should work with the speaker to determine the impact desired.

It is useful, then, to speak of the objective of a speech in terms of change. For every writing assignment, the writer determines the objective of the speech by asking, "How do I expect this audience to be changed by this speech?" The answer should be clear in the writer's mind at all stages of the writing process.

The desired change should be determined in advance, and it should accomplish an objective that serves the legitimate needs of the speaker and the speaker's organization. It is not enough, as Professor William Norwood Brigance once noted, to change members of an audience by making them numb on one end and dumb on the other.

Four specific types of change will be considered here: to give information, to stir feelings, to change minds, and to get action. It may be useful for a writer to think of these four changes as four steps on a stairway starting with information and building to action. The stairway is a valid analogy because the changes are increasingly harder to bring about as you move up the list and also because each step builds on the one that precedes it.

To Give Information

Some speeches succeed if they explain or describe something to an audience. The audience may learn new information, or it may gain new insights into a problem that the listeners already knew something about. Teaching and training are two areas where giving information will frequently be found as a legitimate change to be brought about.

Although it is the simplest and easiest of the four changes to achieve, giving information nevertheless presents a challenge to the writer. The information must be fresh and interesting, and it must, above all, be clear.

Because of the stairstep nature of the changes, writers must know where to stop. They must know when to move on to seek to bring about a more challenging change and when to settle for a lower step on the stairway. To illustrate how choices are made, an example will be offered for each of the steps. In the examples, two factors will be kept constant: the speaker and the subject. The speaker in the examples will be the vice-president of a utility company, and the subject will be "Our New Marketing Plan." The variables will be those facts commonly gathered in audience analysis, the facts that tell the writer which changes are realistic and which are not.

The speech designed to give information will be given to company employees. They have heard rumors of a new, aggressive marketing approach under consideration by top management, but no details have been released. Through careful inquiry, the speech writer has found no strong opposition to the new idea among employees, but at the same time no evidence of strong support for the idea has surfaced. The speech writer urges that the speech to the employees on the new plan be given before information about the proposal reached the general public. To get the word out quickly, the vice-president will speak to half a dozen employee groups over a period of two days. The speech will set forth in detail why the company abandoned its old policy, how the new one will work, and what the company expects to gain.

To Stir Feelings

Sometimes an audience needs a pep talk. In such a case, a speaker moves up one step beyond merely giving information and delivers a speech to stimulate listeners by stirring their feelings. An army general speaking to a ROTC commissioning exercise would not be well advised simply to describe life in the military or to explain how young officers should behave. This occasion calls for a speech to compliment and inspire, to make the graduates feel good about themselves and their new occupation.

Politicians use the speech to stir feelings when they address their supporters. Business executives who agree with one another often meet to hear one of their number damn their enemies and praise their friends. At such events as retirement banquets and building dedications, the speech to stir feelings serves a useful purpose.

To return to the utility company example, the vice-president might seek to stir feelings in an address at the annual luncheon for company speakers' bureau members. At the time of this speech, the company marketing plan has been in effect for a year, and the speakers' bureau has been used as one means to help sell the idea to the public. The speech writer has discovered that the members of the bureau are themselves sold on the plan, and they are proud of their public presentations on the subject. The writer decides to include in the talk specific facts about the speeches given by members of the bureau, and the vice-president will spend twenty minutes telling them what a good job they have done and how much the company appreciates their help.

To Change Minds

One objective of a speech may be to convince an audience that a particular belief should be accepted or rejected. False beliefs held by employees or by the public at large can hurt an organization. Employees who do not believe in company policies may not be as productive as they could be; an erroneous public conviction about a company's safety procedures could lead to unneeded and expensive local laws.

Understanding the nature of the speech to change minds starts with the recognition that there must be a specific issue at stake. The writer should be able to state the issue in the form of a proposition written out as a single complete sentence. The proposition should be one the speaker believes but one the target audience either opposes or has not yet formed an opinion on. Propositions may be of three types.

First is the proposition of fact. In this case, the audience does not accept a factual statement as true. The difference between the speech to give information and the speech to change minds on a proposition of fact is little more than the presence or absence of a conviction in the listener's mind. "We have a new marketing strategy" is a factual statement not likely to be disbelieved. On the other hand, a speaker who argues, "We are not guilty of any of the twelve safety violations alleged in the newspapers'' may be stating a fact very much in doubt.

Second is the proposition of policy. A proposition of policy contends that something should or should not be done. As in all other speeches to convince, the writer should have reason to assume that the audience disagrees with the proposition or has no opinion on it. The speech to change minds on a proposition of policy does not call for any action on the part of listeners. For the speech to be successful, the audience at the end of the speech must simply believe in the soundness of the speaker's view. Speeches arguing that property taxes should be lower or environmental safeguards should be stronger are examples of propositions of policy.

Third are propositions of value. A proposition of value contends that something is good or bad. A speech proclaiming the virtues of the free enterprise system, which would be a speech to stir feelings if given to believers, would be a speech to change minds if given before a dubious audience.

To return to the case of the utility company, the vice-president delivers a speech to change minds to a group of journalism students. The writer's research has determined that a large majority of the students believe utility companies should not advertise or promote their services in any way. Conversations with several of the students and one professor have led the writer to believe the students are not firm in their beliefs. They do not appear to know much about the subject and have not heard an articulate presentation for the opposite view.

The writer therefore decided to build the speech around a proposition of fact: "An aggressive marketing strategy best serves the interest of our company and the public." The speech will give information as it explains the economic conditions that led to the company's decision and reports the results on company finances and customer service. There may be some opportunity to stir feelings of appreciation and respect. But the object of the speech can be found in neither presentation of data nor the stirring of feelings; the speech will be judged a success only if it changes minds.

To Get Action

The speech to change the minds of an audience may have the long-term effect of causing action. A speech calling for lower property taxes may result in listeners' donating time to an antitax campaign or signing a petition to get an issue on the ballot. But it is useful to think of the top step on the stairs as representing the speech that gets action as an immediate, direct result.

Asking the audience to do something is not always appropriate. But, on the other hand, many speeches that should call for action stop short and thus fail to get the optimum result that could have been achieved.

An excellent illustration of a speaker aiming for action can be found in many of the speeches of the Reverend Jesse Jackson. When he was an active candidate for the Democratic nomination for the presidency in 1984, Jackson had a clear strategic goal: to build a stronger base of political power. It logically followed that a subordinate goal was to register voters who would cast their ballots for him in primaries. In speech after speech before audiences that included unregistered supporters, Jackson did not stop with giving facts, stirring feelings, or changing minds (although his speeches appeared to accomplish all of these intermediate goals). Instead he called for action. He asked unregistered voters to raise their hands and then march to the front of the room where they would schedule a time to register.

For a writer to come up with an appropriate action for listeners to take may require considerable ingenuity. But a speech on safety that calls on the audience to fill out a checklist on reducing hazards or to pick up safety stickers to place in critical areas may be more meaningful than a simple speech to stir feelings. When a writer does decide to call for an audience to do something, three characteristics of the action speech should be kept in mind.

First, the action should be clear. The desired action must be specified unambiguously. Many speakers with apparently strong feelings about the issues they discuss frequently fail to tell the audience what to do. Often this failure seems to result from timidity. The speaker dances to the edge of the cliff and then pulls back quickly to avoid taking the plunge. In other cases, the object of the speech has not been thought through carefully, and the speaker does not have a clear idea of what the audience can or ought to do.

An audience can take only a fairly limited number of actions. They can give, volunteer, sign a petition, agree to write a letter, form a committee, and not a great deal more. Whatever the action is, the speaker must set it forth clearly: "So, then, tonight I urge you to join other civic clubs throughout the city in voting to endorse the resolution. I hope to be able to report to the committee that your vote was unanimous."

Second, the action should be easy. The speech writer should make sure that the audience can take the desired action without going to a lot of trouble. This may require some extrarhetorical devices. If a resolution is to be voted on, copies of it ought to be made available. If the action is a donation, envelopes and perhaps pledge cards should be ready for distribution. If the action calls for the writing of letters, the proper mailing addresses should be provided along with a fact sheet on the issues. (A form letter may be advisable in some cases, but original, personal letters are usually better.)

Third, the action should be made necessary. A weak call for action without powerful appeals to the interests of the audience will not often do the job. The speech to get action should not be timid; it should establish a clear connection between arguments developed in the talk and the need to act. The temptation to stop at the level of changing minds should be resisted, and the speech should end with a ringing call for action. Effective instances of a speaker's making the action necessary can be found by listening to a television evangelist plead for money by demonstrating the harm that will come if donations are not made and the good that will result if they are made.

To return to the utility company speech, a good example of the action talk can be seen in the meeting held by the company board of directors on the day they met to vote on the plan. The speech writer had found out that over half the board apparently had no convictions one way or the other on the proposed marketing approach. Twenty-five percent were thought generally to favor a more aggressive company stance; the remaining 25 percent tended to take a conservative stance, at least initially, in regard to almost any policy change. Within the conservative group, two of the board members were known to be strongly opposed to almost every marketing concept the company had ever introduced.

The writer decided that success stories from other utilities that had recently tried similar plans would be the best evidence for the vice-president to use. This information was collected, attractive visuals were prepared to show anticipated growth in income, and a printed summary of the plan was prepared as a handout. The vice-president was briefed to handle the Q&A session that in typical board procedure always came just before the vote. The president of the company made the motion to accept the plan and, with the vice-president still in the room, it passed with two abstentions and no negative votes.

Features of the Stairstep Model

The progression from giving information to stirring feelings to changing minds to getting action is both cumulative and of increasing degrees of difficulty.

The progress is cumulative because, except for the speech to inform, each desired change builds on the ones below it in the model. A speech to stir feelings must inform, and a speech to change minds both gives information and stirs feelings. The speech to get action does all four.

The point to keep in mind is that the speech writer must focus on the ultimate change desired. The intended effect of the speech should always be expressed as a single change. In talking of effect, the word *and* should not be used. It is redundant to think of a speech as having as an objective both to "give information" and "stir feelings." The second change encompasses the first, and to consider both as the object of the speech may have the effect of blurring the focus of the speech.

The concept of cumulative effect rests, however, on an important assumption: it assumes a homogeneous audience. This assumption must be checked in preparing each speech, but it will generally be valid. Audiences, after all, tend to come together because they have something in common. When the assumption does not hold, the writer may decide essentially to ignore one segment of the audience and aim the message at the other segment. In some cases, diehard opposition may be written off so the speech may be directed at neutrals in the audience, while in other cases, partisans of the speaker's cause can be disregarded so the speech can be written only for the unconverted in the audience.

The desired changes will almost always be harder to achieve as the writer moves up the stairsteps. Bringing about any kind of change in an audience will prove difficult enough, but, to cite one simple illustration, it is easier to make someone believe that a charity does commendable work than it is to get that same person to write a check to support the cause.

Writers make two kinds of errors in failing to understand the varied difficulty of speech objectives. In some cases, speeches reach for too much. A writer has little chance of successfully writing a speech trying to change the minds of alarmed members of a home owners' association so they will believe that a chemical dump site in their neighborhood is a wonderful idea. If there is any point in speaking to such a group at all, the speech would have to be a carefully arranged effort to describe the facts.

On the other hand (and this is a far more common problem), speakers go before friendly audiences without daring to do more than belt out another speech designed to stir up feelings. In many cases, a talk calling on the audience to accept a new belief or take a certain action would make better use of the speaker's time.

The speech writer should examine the stairstep model with the intent of climbing as high as possible in a given speech. The more ambitious the goal, if it is also realistic, the greater is the return on the investment of energy and money represented by the speech.

The stairstep model omits two matters that should be mentioned briefly. First, the writer can expect a bonus result over and above the four changes in the model. A friendly feeling of goodwill toward the speaker and the speaker's organization should be an automatic by-product of almost any good speech. We live in a polite society, and audiences appreciate the effort demonstrated in a good speech. In spite of all the humor that abounds about dull speeches, a speaker who does a credible job will earn a measure of appreciation from most audiences.

A second omission, the speech designed to entertain, does not fit appropriately into the model. Because the objective of that type of speech is so unlike the others, it will be dealt with in chapter 7.

CONCLUSION

Donald Bryant has defined public speaking as a process in which ideas are adjusted to people and people are adjusted to ideas. That definition points up the critical role of audience analysis and setting objectives. The audience must be studied with care to learn how the material to be used in the speech can be adjusted to fit its needs and interests. Then the writer must decide how the audience itself is to be adjusted by selecting an appropriate change that the speech should seek to bring about.

4

Organizing Ideas Clearly

> First I tell them what I'm going to tell them. Then I tell them. And then
> I tell them what I've told them
> —Classic formula for organizing a sermon

Along with all its advantages as a medium of communication, speech has
one major disadvantage: it is instantaneous. The message must be grasped
at the moment it is uttered, or the listener fails to get the point. Speech does
not allow a listener the privilege a reader has to put a book down and think
about an idea or even to go back and reread a passage. Therefore speeches
must be organized with particular care to make it easy for listeners to follow
the thoughts. The structure of a speech is not necessarily more rigid or
logical than that of, for instance, a report. But the structure of the speech
must take into account the special needs of listeners.

There is no one perfect formula for organizing a speech. Writers use a
variety of methods, but only one system will be discussed in detail here. The
pattern suggested here rests on the same basic principles found in any well-
organized speech. It permits great flexibility in application so that all
speeches need not sound the same.

The formula has four parts:

I. Opening
II. Thesis Statement
III. Body (with two to five main points)
    A. Main Point
    B. Main Point
    C. Main Point
IV. Close

OPENING

The opening of a speech ordinarily consists of a minute or two of material designed to get the audience in a friendly mood, get the attention and interest of the audience, and begin to orient the audience to the speaker's subject. In some instances, all three of the initial goals may be accomplished at once. A speaker who opens, "I'm here to tell you that everyone's salary will be doubled starting tomorrow," can be expected instantly to have an attentive, friendly, well-oriented audience. Most subjects cannot be introduced so easily; most of the time several different devices are needed in order to accomplish each of the three goals.

An audience may be attentive without being in a good mood, or it may be well oriented but uninterested in the subject. To make sure that all the goals are accomplished, a number of proved techniques can be drawn upon. These techniques form a sort of recipe for preparing a good opening. The instructions are flexible but simple: mix in enough of the techniques to accomplish the required goals for a particular audience.

At the outset of the discussion of techniques for opening a speech, the social nature of the scene for a speech should be noted. Writers need to be aware of the social nature of a speech because speeches are usually prepared in a formal setting quite unlike that in which the speech will be delivered. Writing speeches is work. Piles of facts and figures may be on the desk. The writer may be in a somber mood. But although the degree of formality may vary from speech to speech, speeches are not usually given in a totally business atmosphere. Food and drink may be consumed. The speech is often delivered after working hours have ended. A large number of people are sitting close together and in all likelihood have been talking to one another before the speech. Although they may well be prepared for the speaker to deal with a serious matter, they expect the speech to take into account the social surroundings in which it is to be given.

The Common Bond

Establishing a common bond can work in a speech in the same way it functions at parties and other social occasions in lowering the barriers between speaker and listener. Often when strangers meet, they routinely seek to establish some common ground in the areas of jobs, hobbies, or even problems they share. One frequent conversational opener using the common ground approach is the "Do you know so-and-so?" gambit. Discovering a mutual friend will often be enough to validate one speaker to another.

A speaker before a large audience can find a common bond in something as important as a mutual dedication to a noble cause or as casual as a common interest in the local football team. Humor may be combined with the common bond, as illustrated by Donald Regan's effort to show that, although he was born in Massachusetts and worked in Washington, his place of residence gave him something in common with his Virginia audience. "I'm a Virginian by choice," he said, "and what's even more important, a Virginia tax payer for life" (Regan 1984, 418).

A good common bond can help a speaker accomplish two of the goals of an opening: it perks up attention, and it helps establish a friendly mood.

The Honest Compliment

The compliment is a powerful force in social situations. A warm expression of commendation can spur an employee on to greater effort or even provide a discouraged spouse with incentive to help keep a marriage afloat.

Almost anyone's interest is attracted by a sincere compliment, and we generally develop a friendly attitude toward those who say nice things about us. The key to using this approach in a speech is to find something the speaker genuinely appreciates about the audience. "It's nice to be back in my favorite city" will not do the job unless the speaker's feeling is heartfelt and the audience knows the sentiment is true. A hollow compliment can hurt a speaker's chances for success.

What better than a sincere compliment for an American CEO to use in opening a speech before a group of students in a university in the People's Republic of China? Donald Kendall of PepsiCo used a half-dozen compliments in his opening remarks at Fudan University:

I'm very pleased to be here today, and I'm grateful to President Xie Xide for inviting me to speak with you. It's a great privilege to visit your world renowned university and to participate in a tradition of scholarship and free exchange of ideas that dates back to 1905.

You are very fortunate in having a leader like Doctor Xie. She is an outstanding educator and an inspiration to students and scholars in both China and America. She is also one of those rare individuals who understands both our countries from personal experience.

I believe that we can learn much from men and women whose experience bridges different cultures and countries, and who are committed to establishing the personal relationships that are the foundation for the more formal ties that follow. (Kendall 1986, 475)

Humor

The old practice of starting every speech with two or three hoary jokes has just about ended among successful speakers. But humor still has a place in gaining attention and winning goodwill. A more detailed discussion of humor will be presented in chapter 7, but for now it should be noted that except for speakers who are exceptionally skilled in handling humor, most writers will find a low-key, low-risk approach offers the best chance of reaching the goals of a speech opening. Low-risk humor should meet one simple test: if the audience does not laugh, will the content of the speaker's comment be strong enough in its own right to avoid embarrassment to the speaker? If the answer is yes, the material is safe. If it gets a laugh, fine. If it does not, the speaker has not been made to look foolish.

When low-risk humor elicits an audience response, the writer should consider it a success even when that response is only a smile, chuckle, or maybe even just a spark of interest in a listener's eye. The purpose of humor in a speech, whether in the opening or elsewhere, is not to get laughter as an end in itself. Low-risk humor has the capacity to accomplish any one of the goals of a speech opening. It can build a friendly climate, it can attract and hold attention, and it can orient the audience by illuminating an idea.

The president of a life insurance company addressing a group of important business executives and community leaders decided to open with a touch of self-effacing humor. Whether or not the audience laughed, the humor clearly served to win a friendly and attentive response. Robert MacDonald of ITT Life Insurance Corporation said:

I'm going to have to ask you to bear with me today. You see, I spend a lot of my time speaking. This means I seldom listen. The end result is—I'm highly uneducated. Unfortunately, this is a fact that will become painfully apparent to all of you shortly. But please give me credit for having wisdom. Because most of my talks are to insurance executives where this deficiency goes unnoticed.

But regardless of the audience, I have found that it can be a bit difficult to capture the imagination of my listeners when they discover I'm in the life insurance business. It seems to me the best way to clear a crowded room wouldn't be to yell, "Fire," but rather, "Life Insurance." (MacDonald 1985, 413)

The Opening Story

Including a story in the opening can strike a friendly chord or orient an audience to the theme of the speech. But the most powerful value of a story will often be its capacity to get an audience's attention. A story has a built-in curiosity factor; most listeners stay tuned in to see how it turns out. The variety of incidents that can be used makes this device highly flexible. It may be taken from personal experience, it may be borrowed from someone else, or it may be purely hypothetical. The tone may be serious or humorous. A story may be suitable to begin an in-house speech on safety or to start a major address as can be seen in the opening of the speech made by Lester Pearson in accepting a Nobel Peace Prize:

I remember one poignant illustration of the futility and tragedy of war. It was concerned . . . with civilian destruction in London in 1941 during its ordeal by bombing. It was a quiet Sunday morning after a shattering night of fire and death. I was walking past the smoking ruins of houses that had been bombed and burned during the night. The day before they had been a neat row of humble, red brick workingmen's dwellings. They were now rubble except for the front wall of one building which may have been some kind of community club and on which there was a plaque that read, "Sacred to the memory of the men of Alice Street who died for peace during the Great War, 1914-1918." The children and grandchildren of those men of Alice Street had now in their turn been sacrificed in the Great War, 1939-1945. For Peace? There are times when it does not seen so. (Pearson 1957, 4)

Reference to the Subject

Most audiences are not ready to hear the substance of what a speaker has to say in the early moments of the opening of a speech. They are getting settled in their chairs, finishing a cup of coffee, or adjusting to the sight and sound of the speaker. A speech, then, usually requires a soft opening; the use of an information-loaded sentence such as that often found in the lead of a good news article generally will not work well.

Some speakers omit reference to the subject in the opening and first reveal the content of the speech in the thesis sentence. Other speakers refer to the subject in the opening of the speech but find it advisable to hold the reference until after one or two other devices have been used. Also, a reference to the subject can be softened by combining it with one of the other techniques already mentioned.

In the speech by Robert MacDonald already cited, the speaker began with low-risk humor. By the time he was ready to refer to his subject, he continued in a light vein:

But you can relax. I'm not here to try to convince you to buy life insurance. I'm here to welcome you to the Peace Conference. Perhaps you hadn't considered yourselves delegates to a peace conference or even realized that a war was going on. It's a war without trumpets or drums, without artillery or B-52s—a silent war.

I'm referring to the Armageddon between the two giant industries of financial services—insurance and banking. I don't come here proposing that the hot war simply cool down to a cold war or become an armed truce with the two sides glaring at each other. Nor am I simply proposing a bilateral freeze.

I do come waging peace. (MacDonald 1985, 413)

Alternatives

In addition to the five major techniques for opening a speech, a number of seldom-used approaches might also be considered. A speech can begin with a startling statement, for example, or with a rhetorical question. If a writer is not careful, however, these methods may appear to demand rather than to deserve attention. The same criticism may be made against the speaker who opens with a gimmick. While this device can be effective, it takes a certain kind of speaker to capitalize on the attention gained by starting a speech on litter by dumping a bag of roadside trash on the floor in front of a startled audience.

Stacking

Although the techniques to be used in the opening of a speech have been treated individually, it is clear that they can be stacked, a single sentence or paragraph in a speech may employ several of the techniques at the same time. Combining of techniques may be readily seen in the following case history.

Case History: Opening Techniques

John Hanley of Monsanto consistently makes effective use of the five techniques for opening a speech. The techniques never become stale because his openings are always tailored in a fresh and lively way to fit each audience he addresses. A sample Hanley opening appears below. It is from a speech delivered before Town Hall of California in Los Angeles, and a quick glance at the passage will show that it makes use of all five of the techniques.

This year marks an anniversary of sorts for me in Los Angeles. Exactly thirty years ago, I came here to start my career as a soap salesman. Five days after I arrived, I met a lovely young Beverly Hills girl, and within a few months she was, somewhat shyly, selling soap and helping me win a sales contest. For the 29 years since, as Mrs. Hanley, she has been my confidant and co-worker.

So, as you can see, I have reason for fond memories of this city and its people.

I want to thank all of you for taking certain risks to come here this afternoon. Let me hasten to add I don't mean by this, to disparage your wonderful freeways. But whether you drove—with or without seatbelts—or whether you simply walked across a street or two, there was an element of risk involved.

I don't say this facetiously. It's an unfortunate fact that there is an element of risk in everything we do. And it is with a keen awareness of this fact that I chose as my topic, "Why Ban Reason From the Consumer Safety Debate?"

Frankly, I have become increasingly concerned about what seems to me an atmosphere of crisis and hysteria surrounding consumer safety. The debate over what is safe, and what regulations are needed to enforce safety, is growing daily in volume and intensity, but regrettably, not in reasonableness and rationality. This year is shaping up as the biggest ever for the wholesale banishment of suspect goods from the marketplace. The saccharin case is likely to be a forerunner of a series of potential future decisions about the marketability of food products.

I'm grateful to have this opportunity to contribute another perspective on this subject—and to do so before Town Hall, which has a richly deserved reputation for its steadfast commitment to public dialogue as an instrument for setting future directions for our nation.

I want to speak to you today about the role you and I can play in putting reason back into the consumer safety debate. (Hanley 1977, 1)

Paragraph 1 combines a story with a common bond and has a hint of a compliment thrown in. A more direct compliment appears in paragraph 2. Paragraphs 3, 4, and 5 refer to the subject with a touch of humor.

Paragraph 6 once again compliments the audience, and paragraph 7, which is not part of the opening proper, sets forth the theme of the speech in a thesis statement.

This opening, which lasts about two minutes, can reasonably be expected to have made the audience attentive, friendly, and fully aware of the theme of the speech. The illustration in paragraph 1 claims attention with an element of personal drama while at the same time it reminds the audience of a past bond and compliments them for having such a fine city. By the time the speaker reaches paragraph 6, the use of the compliment becomes direct and straightforward. The use of humor in paragraph 3 is low risk, and the reference to the subject in paragraphs 3, 4, and 5 comes only after all of the other techniques have already been used.

THESIS STATEMENT

After the opening of the speech, the next step is to state the central idea of the speech in a sentence or two. The audience should know in advance what the speech will cover so they will not have to puzzle over the relevance of the points and the evidence in the body of the talk. A writer for print media may enjoy the flexibility of providing data that lead up to a point, but a speech writer will often find that this places too great a burden on listeners. A direct initial statement of the thrust of the complete speech can be seen in the final paragraph quoted from the Hanley talk.

Some writers extend this statement of thesis, the "tell them what you are going to tell them" section of the talk, to include a preview of the main points. For example, speaking to a conference on innovation, the CEO of Smith-Kline Corporation set forth his thesis with the statement, "I would like to cover three points. The first deals with the meaning of innovation. The second with the environment in which it can be expected to flourish. And the third with the state of innovation in the United States today" (Dee 1979, 2-3).

BODY OF THE SPEECH

In the body of the speech, the writer should develop two to five main ideas that support the thesis statement. Ideally the audience should know at any given time during the speech exactly which point is being developed, and at the end of the speech, the audience should know how many points were presented, as well as the ideas the points expressed.

Patterns

When a writer begins to put together the body of a speech, the material to be included will ordinarily be scattered about. One fact will be in a report, another in a magazine article, yet another in the writer's notes. This random material must be put in order.

The concept of main points provides a means for an intelligent grouping of data. The concept rests on the assumption that mere facts do not speak for themselves; their relevance must be established so the audience can see how they support the points or claims made in the speech. These are the points that in turn support the thesis, and their number must be held within reasonable limits so they do not strain the mental powers of listeners.

Sometimes, of course, the preparation of the speech starts with the points because the speaker ticks off a list of broad ideas to be covered. But when the writer starts with only a theme, it will usually prove helpful to experiment with various patterns to see which pattern offers the best arrangement of points.

These patterns can be used to organize into a logical sequence the main points of a speech and any subpoints that may be necessary. The main points should follow a single consistent pattern, as should any given set of subpoints, but the pattern for the main points does not have to be the same as the pattern for the subpoints.

Time. Speaking before the Texas legislature, Michael Stewart discussed problems in relationships between state and local governments. The two points he developed in calling for improvements can be found in the words of the subtitle of his speech, "Present and Future Tensions" (Stewart 1985, 662). As this speech demonstrates, facts in a speech may be rationally grouped in a chronological sequence.

Du Pont's Irving Shapiro also used two points in time order to express his ideas on "The Lawyer's Special role" (Shapiro 1979, 258-61). He discussed the lawyer's role first through some history and then used the second half of his speech to consider the role of the lawyer today.

These two speeches illustrate selective use of past, present, and future as points for a speech. A writer may use all three or may use a simple chronological series of steps such as "the first phase of the operation, the second phase of the operation, and the third phase. . . ." Time order gives an audience a sequence of ideas that can be easily grasped.

Space. Points may sometimes be produced by grouping facts according to space or geography. This system makes ideas especially easy for an audience to visualize and keep in order. The clarity of ideas presented in space order may be seen in a telephone industry speech of a few years ago. The thesis of the speech was to explain the long-distance telephone network. The first point discussed long-distance telephone communication by land, and the second dealt with transmission by undersea cable. It is easy to see that many members of the audience would have found the third point a logical extension of the first two: long-distance communication through the air by satellite.

In a speech evaluating the problems of the transfer of United States technology, W. S. Anderson, chairman of NCR, employed two main points built on a geographical distinction. He first considered problems of technology transfer from West to East, the free world to the communist bloc, and then turned his attention to technology transfer from North to South, the developed to the so-called developing nations (Anderson 1977, 1-13). Once again the ideas in a speech on a complex topic were made easy to follow.

Topical. By far the most common pattern of main points in speeches is a division based on breaking a subject down into its logical or natural topics. In the speech on technology transfer, the speaker might have chosen to substitute for the spatial points a set of points consisting of economic, political, and military implications of technology transfer. The time order used in the Shapiro speech on lawyers could have been changed to topical order by using such points as the role of the lawyer as adviser and the role of the lawer as advocate.

Topical dividision of ideas served David Rockefeller well in a speech, "The Chief Executive in the Year 2000," delivered to the Commonwealth Club of California (Rockefeller 1980, 162-64). Using a preview of his main points immediately after the statement of his thesis, Rockefeller stated his three topical points:

This afternoon I'd like to take a step [toward planning for the future] by covering three areas. First, elaborate a bit more on why I think it's critical that you and I start paving the way for the development of the managers of the next century. Second, discuss several of the environmental challenges that those managers might face, and, third, offer a brief "character sketch" of the manner of man or woman I think will be effective in what promises to be a brave, new corporate world.

In another example, John Hanley's "Lessons I've Learned since Graduation" also has three topical points. Here is how the points appear, not in the preview but in the body of the speech: "Lesson No. 1: Cultivate your curiosity," "This brings me to Lesson No. 2: Enlarge your enthusiasm," and "That's Lesson No. 3: Make the law of averages work for you" (Hanley 1981, 598-600).

Speaking to a health industry group in Washington, Karl Bays made his ideas stand out clearly with topical points (Bays 1986, 184-85):

It seems to me that there are three major concerns. I'll list them not just as priorities but as obligations for us. I'll take them one by one. [Thesis]

The first is the need to create equity, and I mean that literally . . . to create equity. I also put it purposely at the head of the list. . . . [First main point]

Now, the second item for our agenda . . . the second obligation that I suggest we share . . . follows immediately from the first. It's the obligation of quality. . . . [Second main point]

Technology [which has just been discussed] also speaks to the third and final item for our agenda. That obligation is progress. [Third main point]

All the examples quoted have three points, and three will often prove to be an appropriate number of ideas to cover in twenty minutes. But the number of points should be determined by the material available, and two or four or five points can be effective when using the topical pattern.

Problem-Solution. Organizing the points of a speech into a problem-solution pattern dictates that there will be only two main points. Problem-solution makes it easy for an audience to follow a speaker who wants to say, "Here's what I think is wrong, and here's what I think we should do about it."

Gale Klappa of Southern Company Services used this approach in his speech, "Journalism and the Anti-Media Backlash." The discussion of the problem of backlash consumed a little more than half the speech, and then the speaker introduced his solution with the statement, "Considering how dangerous this anti-media backlash could be, we must ask ourselves—what can we do?" (Klappa 1985, 376-78).

In a variation on the problem-solution pattern, John Ong of BFGoodrich first explored the difficulties faced by the tire industry and then attacked a much-discussed solution that he did not believe would work. He previewed his points in his thesis sentence with the statement, "Let's examine the problem and then return to this so-called solution" (Ong 1980, 112).

Using the Patterns Creatively

Any one of the four patterns can be used to write a dull speech. Having three clear points in topical order does little for a speech that lacks substance. And writers want to avoid falling into a rut by making each successive speech fit a repetitive pattern that may not always set off the speaker's ideas to best advantage.

But the patterns can be used creatively. Consider the variety possible with the single topic. A speech on the environment, for example, might significantly aid an audience's understanding of the topic if it presents, in chronological order, an insightful analysis of the eras through which concern for the environment has passed. A fresh view of the situation might emerge from a speech looking at the same ideas with points arranged from a geographic perspective. If the writer chose to use topical order, a great variety of divisions become apparent. These could range from the obvious categories of air, water, and noise to a sophisticated presentation of aesthetic, economic, and social perspectives of the problem.

The writer should feel no obligation to exhaust every conceivable feature of the subject. A speech can legitimately carve out an announced segment of an issue and deal with that segment alone. In deciding exactly what material to use, the writer who toys with the various possible patterns of organization will discover a healthy number of choices. Far from getting a writer into a repetitious rut, experimentation with the patterns will often suggest new and exciting ways to treat ideas. The organizational process can and should be a creative one.

Making Main Points Stand Out

Having a clearly delineated set of main points is the first step in making it possible for an audience to follow and remember a speaker's ideas. In addition to having ideas in the speech arranged systematically, the writer will ordinarily wish to make sure that the points emerge forcefully during speech delivery. Although the ideas on the pages of the manuscript may be in a strict logical pattern, that fact alone does not guarantee that a listener, again because of the instantaneous nature of speech, will be able to follow the movement from one concept to another.

Following a few simple guidelines will improve the chances that the main points of a speech will stand out clearly for the listeners. Some of the suggestions may appear heavy-handed to an editor of a newspaper or a company magazine. Such an editor should realize that readers of print benefit from many nonverbal clues that alert readers to changes from one idea to another on the page. The clues include paragraphs, varied size and boldness of type, and use of white space. The speech writer appreciates the fact that the audience has no manuscript before it and thus needs to hear the clues that announce a switch from one concept to the next.

Label the Points. No simpler way can be found to identify points clearly than to number them. "First," "second," and "third" or "number one," "number two," and "number three" will do the job. Variations, such as Hanley's "Lesson No. 1" and "Lesson No. 2," can grow out of the nature of the material in the speech. Writers should try to avoid overusing the word *point* following the label. Substitutions include "My first concern. . . . My second concern," "The first obstacle. . . . The second obstacle," "Our first obligation. . . . Our second obligation."

To avoid confusion, one method of labeling may be necessary for main points and another for subpoints so listeners are spared a barrage of "firsts" and "seconds." Writers should be careful as they move from draft to draft of a speech that they leave behind no dangling firsts where succeeding ideas were edited out. Otherwise listeners may think more about what was cut from a speech than they do about what was left in.

State the Point. A writer for print may proceed to give facts without stating the point that the writer's facts support. The point in such a case may be printed in a heading outside the text proper, or it may be revealed in the middle of the material or at the end. Readers can handle this manner of writing better than can listeners, who must absorb the data and then upon learning the point engage in a mental review to see if the material fits the idea. While the rule is not inflexible, for a speaker may sometimes withhold a point, writers as a rule are well advised to spell out each point in a simple sentence before presenting supporting data.

A good example of succinctly stated points appears in the speech on the three lessons by Hanley. Not counting his numbers, Hanley used fourteen words to make three points, each of which was expressed in a complete sentence. For another example, Thomas Shannon, speaking to the New York State School Boards Association, posed the question of what his audience could do to "maintain and nurture excellence" in education. He answered the question in his thesis statement: "The answer is: plenty! All you need are the 'smarts' and the 'guts' to do it!" He turned to his first main point, "Let's talk first about the 'smarts,'" and halfway through the speech moved to his second point by stating, "[This] can be done if we have the 'guts' to ask the right questions" (Shannon 1986, 207-9). It would be hard to imagine anyone leaving the speech unable to recall the speaker's two main ideas.

Writers may be especially reluctant to state the first point of a speech when that point follows immediately after a preview. They apparently fear they will be guilty of talking down to the audience. That risk is small; the greater fault is not to be understood. A thesis with a preview and a first point would look like this if the guidelines were followed:

So today I offer you my three keys to getting ahead. Work hard, learn from mistakes, and never cheat. [Thesis with preview]
   Let's look at that first key, work hard. [First main point]

Use Previews and Summaries. The preview as a part of the thesis statement has already been discussed. The examples presented are quite straightforward, but a preview does not have to be mechanical. Consider the thesis and preview found in the Lester Pearson Nobel Prize Address, an address the speaker entitled, "The Four Faces of Peace." Pearson said:

Our problem then, so easy to state; so hard to solve—is how to bring about a creative peace and a security which will have a strong foundation. There have been thousands of volumes written by the greatest thinkers of the ages on this subject, so you will not expect too much from me in a few sketchy and limited observations. I cannot, I fear, provide you, in the words of Alfred Nobel, with "some lofty thoughts to lift us to the spheres."
   My aim this evening is a more modest one. I wish to look at the problem in four of its aspects—my "four faces of peace." There is Peace and Trade, Peace and Power, Peace and Policy, or Diplomacy, [and] Peace and People. (Pearson 1957, 5)

A summary may occur in the conclusion of the speech. A useful application of the summary in the body of the speech, however, calls for a recapitulation of ideas perhaps half or two-thirds the way through. "What have we seen so far?" the speaker asks, and then briefly summarizes points A, B, and C before moving on to D and E.

Add Transitions. The speech writer, and sometimes the speaker, gets to know a speech manuscript so well it is easy to forget how complex the ideas will be to an audience. Supplying transitions from one idea to another makes it easier for listeners to keep up. The transitions can be simple: "But let us consider another matter" or "Moving on now" or "Turning to an even more pressing issue." Transitions have their place in both writing and speaking, but they are especially needed in speaking.

Anita Taylor at the midpoint of her speech, "Women as Leaders," combined an internal summary of her first point with a smooth transition to her second point:

Thus, I have explicated half my thesis: Leadership now and in the future will require many skills for which women are uniquely qualified. [Internal summary]

There is another half. [Transition] Women will be able to provide leadership only if they acquire some specific communication skills and shed some attitudes that currently inhibit them. [Second point]

Parallel Phrasing. Using parallel sentence structure for main points will make them stand out. A speaker might say, "If we want to save the world, we must, first . . ." and "If we want to save the world, we must, second, . . ."

Other Devices. Writers may resort to having the first letters of key words in each point spell out a word, as when a speech called "Your Speakers Bureau Can Hit the SPOT," uses the words *support, purpose, organization,* and *training* to spell *SPOT."* Or a writer may attempt to have the audience associate each point with some visual image: "Let's look at the speech writer in two ways: the speech writer sitting at the keyboard and the speech writer sitting in the audience." Rhyming words can be used to make the points: "Today we will compare and contrast 'Education to learn' and 'Education to earn.'" Any of these devices must be used with care to avoid letting the technique overshadow or even distort the message.

Do Not Dawdle. Many writers begin the body of a speech hesitantly. Often after a ringing statement of the let-me-tell-you-how-to-restore-our-leadership sort, these writers suddenly get cold feet. The next statement, instead of moving boldly into the first idea in support of the thesis, says something like, "But before we go further, we need to explore the history of the subject." Usually such a tentative toe-in-the-water start is little more than a stall. Whatever material the writer has in the stalling segment can be plucked out and placed either in the opening or in one of the main points.

The direct approach used by Thomas Horton in "Winning in the Global Marketplace" usually works best: "Tonight I'd like to address three basic points,'' Horton stated, and then moved without delay to his inital point, "First, I'd like to suggest that there are good, indeed compelling, reasons to try to win the global marketplace" (Horton 1986, 392).

Exceptions. Not all speeches, not even all good speeches, leave the audience with the points clearly in mind as separate ideas. Usually a good speech that lacks distinct main points of the sort discussed will nevertheless be organized in a logical pattern. Lincoln's Gettysburg Address, for example, does not have three clear main points; however, the most cursory reading of the speech reveals a sound structure in chronological order moving from past ("Forescore and seven years ago") to present (the longest section, "Now we are engaged") and future ("this nation, under God, shall have a new birth of freedom").

When a speech does not have clear main points, it should be because the writer made a conscious decision not to make the points stand out. It should not be because the writer lacked the technique or the skill to leave ideas firmly planted in the listeners' minds. Even when the devices for making the points stand out are missing, the speech will almost always benefit from following a strict logical order. It will be much easier, for example, to make the best use of data if the points at issue are at least clear to the writer even though the audience may not be able to pick them out on a multiple-choice test after the speech.

SPEECH CONCLUSION

Conclusions should be short. When an audience detects from either the content of the talk or the tone of the speaker's voice that the speech is about to end, the speaker can expect to hold attention for about another thirty seconds or perhaps up to a minute. An ending that drags on much more than a minute can undo much of the positive impression of an otherwise good speech.

Conclusions should not routinely end with the all-too-common "thank you." In the first place, the audience thanks the speaker at the end of a speech, not the other way around. In the second place, should there be a valid reason for the speaker to express thanks to an audience, two words would hardly do it. A statement of thanks would take at least a sentence or two. For example, GM's Roger Smith no doubt left his audience feeling good when he concluded a speech with a substantive statement of appreciation as the final part of his conclusion: "I thank you again for your invitation. I hope your conference is productive and stimulating, and that its rewards are felt long after it has ended" (Smith 1984, 635).

Only one excuse totally justifies ending with "thank you." If the speech is weak or the speaker poor at delivery, the "thank you" has the effect of sending the universal signal, "That's all, folks," and can thus avoid some awkwardness at the end of the talk. If speakers insist on ending with "thank you" in otherwise good speeches, the writer should try to treat these two words as a throwaway line. The speech should have a strong ending that will not be undercut by the weak ending. Still, it's hard to imagine Lincoln at Gettysburg or Patrick Henry in St. John's Church following their rousing conclusions with a "thank you."

Ending a Speech

Summary. A summary in the form of a restatement of points or by repeating the thesis can be a valuable means of getting the message of a speech concisely before the audience at the conclusion of a speech. Having stated in his thesis sentence that he saw a "very rosy economic picture for the future," George Marotta ended a Kiwanis Club speech with a restatement of that thesis: "In sum, the big stock market story is that the American economy is getting back on a long-term growth pattern after a dangerous 13-year flirtation with inflation. Now the stock market is saying, 'Let the good times roll'" (Marotta 1986, 308).

Quotation. A well-stated sentiment that captures the essence of the speech can provide a solid ending. David Mahoney ended a speech before the American Association of Advertising Agencies by making a quotation part of his close:

I have one more thought that will put my remarks in perspective. It's a quote from Malcolm Muggeridge, the British writer and social critic, who once said "There is no such thing as darkness; only the failure to see." We in the business community are playing not to lose, instead of playing to win. Let's play to win. (Mahoney 1978, 448)

Challenge. In the close of the Mahoney speech, the two sentences following the quotation offer a good example of a challenge to the audience as part of the conclusion of a speech. Patrick Henry's "Give me liberty or give me death" may be the best-known challenge ending an address, but here are a number of final sentences taken from just one issue of *Vital Speeches* (August 15, 1981): "May we all rise to the challenge ahead!" "Harvest a new era in agriculture . . . with more production and less consumption." "Let us get back to the basic job of making America America again—this time for everyone!" "You can count on it!" "Let's do it!"

Illustration. Just as a story may be used to start a speech, it may be used to end one. Writers tend to overlook this highly effective way of bringing a speech to a close. Edward Crutchfield demonstrated how it can work:

Let me leave you with a hard lesson learned many years ago. I played a little football once for Davidson—a small men's college about 20 miles north of Charlotte. One particularly memorable game for me was one in which I was blindsided on an off-tackle trap. Even though that was 17 years ago, I can still recall the sound of crackling bones ringing in my ears. Well, 17 years and three operations later my back is fine. But I learned something important about competition that day. Don't always assume that your competition is straight in front of you. It's easy enough to be blindsided by a competitor who comes at you from a very different direction. (Crutchfield 1980, 537)

Rhythm of the Conclusion

The final line of a good conclusion to a speech should have a definite beat in the rhythm of the words. The writer should read aloud an early draft to make sure the pulse is right. An example of an irregular beat that produces a weak ending can be seen by removing two words from Patrick Henry's famous closing line. "Give me liberty or . . . death" keeps all the ideas, but it has lost Henry's powerful rhythm.

Many writers choose an ending quotation from a poem to give a speech a satisfactory flow of language at the end. But prose can do the job even though it may approach the rhythm of poetry. An example where the distinction was blurred may be seen in the close of Ronald Reagan's Second Inauguration Address, when he said, "God bless you and may God bless America."

Speaking at Harvard University, New York governor Mario Cuomo demonstrated one of the strengths of his ability as a speaker with a close that has something of the beat of a college cheer in the challenge of his final lines:

As you go, Harvard, so will go students all over America.
So, in the words of a great American, go for it!
All of you.
Go for and with each other.
Go against oppression and despair and indifference and lowered aspirations.
Go with the certainty that your one life can make a difference and that together you can shake and shape this country and the world.
Go for it, Harvard.
And go for it now! (Cuomo 1985, 584)

CONCLUSION

The vast majority of modern speeches do not measure up to the standards of organization proposed here. Often ideas are not written in logical order, and even when they are, the language of the speech frequently fails to make ideas emerge clearly enough to be grasped by listeners. Many times these failures weaken the impact of the speeches.

Whatever the state of current speaking, our society still prizes logical analysis and clarity of thought. A sound organizational pattern will impress an audience and make a speech writer's job a lot simpler.

5

Using Data to Support Ideas Effectively

[A fact is] nothing. It is valuable only for the idea attached to it, or for the proof which it furnishes.

—Claude Bernard

There is a popular radio preacher who speaks with a sense of urgency in a commanding voice. He poses questions of great magnitude and can keep an audience spellbound for a quarter of an hour. But a critical listener will soon discover that the material in the sermon does not hang together. Apart from the preacher's compelling delivery, his secret seems to be that he allows his listeners to translate his mixture of assertions and miscellaneous bits of information to fit whatever theological views they happen to hold.

IDENTIFICATION OF CLAIMS

Few speakers can get away with the trick of having no significant content, and none should try. If a speaker decides to expend the resources necessary to give a speech, it ought to have something to say. That "something to say" should be subjected to two questions as the speech is being prepared. First, what claim or claims does the speech advance, and second, what evidence can be produced to back up any claim being made?

Let us look first at the notion of a claim. There is nothing wrong with a speech expressing an opinion or making an assertion. That essentially is what a claim is. The speaker regards the claim as important and wants the audience to think of it the same way.

The place to begin the search for claims is in the thesis statement of a talk.

A speaker says, "So I want to explain how government regulation strangles economic growth" or "If the Widget industry is to survive, we must increase productivity" or "Television is poisoning the minds of our youth."

Implied Claims

In a surprising number of cases, speakers imply rather than express the claims they make. All of the claims just cited might well have appeared in camouflage: "Let's take a look at the significant relationship between government regulation and economic growth" or "I want to examine the progress the Widget industry has made in improving productivity" or "We must ask ourselves what effect television is having on the minds of our youth."

Claims may be made implicit rather than explicit in some cases because the audience would be startled or even offended by a blunt statement of the speaker's case. There is nothing necessarily dishonest about the approach; it assumes that if the audience starts with an open mind, the speaker will have a chance to make a reasonable case for the claim. In many cases, claims are implied because of what we might call social custom. The speaker starts off indirectly for the same reason a clerk in a store asks "May I help you?" rather than "May I sell you something?"

The writer must identify the implied claim. Usually it will be obvious. When it is not—and this may be the case rather often, with the subordinate claims to be examined later—the claim should actually be written out. This may be done conveniently by penciling the claim in the manuscript in double brackets so the stated claim and the implied claim appear on the page. The double brackets identify the implied claim for the speech writer and should not appear in the final manuscript.

A 1979 speech that had as its thesis "to assess business conditions" demonstrates an interesting case where the speaker supplied his audience with implied claims and immediately made the claims explicit. Speaking at Southern Methodist University's School of Business, John McGillicuddy, chairman of Manufacturers Hanover, previewed his main points this way:

First, the immediate economic outlook, *which I do not see as nearly so bleak as sometimes portrayed.* Second, the impact on economic growth of the latest OPEC increases—*painful for many countries, including our own, but fully manageable.* Third, some observations on the President's energy proposals, *which I find encouraging in some respects, disappointing in others.* Finally, I will close [with] some personal observations." (McGillicuddy 1979, 706; emphasis supplied to set off the stated claims in the first three points)

Subordinate Claims

When a writer uses the organizational scheme described in chapter 4, the thesis sentence will establish the central claim made in the speech. That claim will be supported in the body of the speech by the main points, which are subordinate claims. Yet another level of subordinate claims may be present if main points are broken down further into subpoints. The writer must identify the links in a chain of claims to make sure that each subordinate claim has a logical relationship to the broader claim under which it falls.

Taking as an example the speech, "Government Regulation: Slow Death for Free Enterprise," by Raymond Tower (Tower 1980, 676-80), this relationship may be readily traced. The thesis of the speech, the first main point, and the first set of subpoints are outlined below. In those instances where the speaker implied the claim, an expressed claim has been supplied in double brackets:

THESIS: "I intend to talk to you today about the subject of excessive government regulation and particularly what I see as a possible outcome, the strangulation of our free enterprise system."

MAIN POINT I: "Let's look at the attack on the free enterprise system." [[Excessive regulation is expensive, overwhelming, and ill motivated.]]

SUBPOINT A: "Business discussion on the regulatory assault often focuses on the costs we're forced to pay." [[Regulation is expensive both directly and indirectly.]]

SUBPOINT B: "Our daily headlines read like the hospital chart of a very sick patient—all the vital signs are moving in the wrong direction. But what concerns me most is the range of foes pitted against the survival of the patient." [[Regulators and their supporters are numerous.]]

SUBPOINT C: "The current regulatory assault is moralistic; it's self-righteous; it's emotional; it's naive."

SUB-SUBPOINT 1: "I say it's profoundly moralistic."

SUB-SUBPOINT 2: "I say that the current onslaught is self-righteous."

SUB-SUBPOINT 3: "I say that the current movement is highly emotional."

SUB-SUBPOINT 4: "I say it's naive."

These, then, are the claims in the first point of a particular speech. Some of the claims are explicit ("I say it's naive") and some implied ("Let's look at the nature of the attack"). With the claims located, the next matter of concern is an examination of the characteristics of claims. That examination will make it apparent why and how claims need to be supported.

Two Characteristics of Claims

Two sets of responses are possible when a claim is presented. First, a listener may understand or may not understand a claim. Of course, there are degrees of understanding. An audience willing to sit through a speech on widget productivity probably has some notion of what the speaker means in claiming it must be improved. But if the audience's understanding is not up to the standard desired by the speaker, then the claim is not understood.

Second, a claim may be believed or not believed. The speaker's hope is to have the audience at the same level of belief as the speaker by the end of the talk. If the aim of the speech is to inform, audience belief should not be an issue. If the aim of the speech is to stimulate, it is assumed that the audience already holds the belief and merely needs to be stirred up.

The writer undertakes the task of making claims understandable and believable by supplying supporting material or evidence. This support must directly follow any claim that comes at the end of a chain of claims. The thesis statement of a speech, then, does not need immediate supporting evidence. The thesis is supported by the main points—the subordinate claims. (The Tower speech does have material intervening between the thesis and the main point. This material, omitted from the above outline, supports the importance of the theme. This type of argument is usually not useful.)

In the Tower speech, main point I is built on subpoints, so it is not at the end of a chain and does not need support. Subpoints A and B are not further subdivided and must be supported. Subpoint C does not need direct evidence to support it, but the four subordinate claims on which it depends for clarity and acceptability must be backed up with evidence.

TYPES OF SUPPORTING MATERIAL

Writers have available five primary types of supporting material: the example, the illustration, the analogy, statistics, and quotations. Based on the circumstances in which the speech is given, the writer can determine the combination of types of support needed to make claims believable and clear to the audience.

The Example

A specific instance can offer convincing proof of a claim. A specific instance, or example, is one concrete case presented briefly. An example can be especially good in supporting a claim that attacks a broad generalization:

CLAIM: It's not true that you have to be a lawyer to get ahead in politics.

EXAMPLE: Look at Reagan and Carter.

Raymond Tower made excellent use of examples in backing up several of his claims. When he asserted that regulators and their supporters are numerous ("a range of forces"), he quickly cited four groups and three names of individuals: "the consumerists and environmentalists, the Friends of the Earth and the Foes of Nuclear Energy" and "the Ralph Naders, Mark Greens, and Jane Fondas."

In supporting his claim that business needs good communicators, Northwestern Bell's Richard McCormick quickly supplied four examples to a group of teachers (McCormick 1984, 52):

We have to be able to tell one another, clearly and concisely, what we're learning from our customers.

We have to be able to sell our ideas to one another, on how to best serve those customers.

We have to be able to sell our products and services.

We have to be able to persuade legislators and regulators that federal rulings have changed the game and state-level changes must follow.

The Illustration

The parables of the Bible and the stories of Abraham Lincoln offer strong proof of the value of telling a story to make a point. Lincoln's tales were often comic and the parables were always serious, but the effect in either case was to make an idea clear. Many times an illustration will not stand up under close scrutiny as logical evidence for a claim, but if other support is available for that purpose, the illustration serves a writer well in helping listeners understand.

In his Inaugural Address of January 20, 1981, President Ronald Reagan advanced the claim that the United States is a nation of heroes "with every right to dream heroic dreams." He called attention to military heroes buried beneath "simple white markers" at nearby Arlington National Cemetery, and he cited examples of battlefields to drive home his point. Then he turned to an illustration for further support:

Under such a marker lies a young man, Martin Treptow, who left his job in a small town barber shop in 1917 to go to France with the famed Rainbow Division. There, on the Western front, he was killed trying to carry a message between battalions under heavy artillery fire. We are told that on his body was found a diary. On the flyleaf under the heading, "My Pledge," he had written these words: "America must win this war. Therefore I will work, I will save, I will sacrifice, I will endure, I will fight cheerfully and do my utmost, as if the issue of the whole struggle depended on me alone."

Returning to the Tower speech, one of the claims was that the attack on the free enterprise system is wrongly motivated. To support that claim, Tower made a subordinate claim that the attack grows out of emotion rather than facts. He backed up the last claim in his chain of arguments by supplying an illustration:

I say that the current movement is highly emotional and often without factual basis [claim]. I imagine many of you saw the recent *National Geographic* article on "The Pesticide Dilemma," a depressing example of the emotionalism I'm talking about. It opened, you will recall, with a moving story about an itinerant worker believed to be dying from exposure to pesticide-related carcinogens. It went on to chronicle abuses in pesticide use and alleged harmful effects, without mentioning the enormous beneficial advances made in controlling pests, improving yields and increasing needed food supplies. The story closed on an unrelated and sensationalist note, speculating that the dying worker's daughter would one day be sorry she now romped in the sun through the fields when she, too, succumbed to her father's fatal affliction. And this, from one of the more distinguished journals in our country!

This illustration could have been shortened to an example just as any of the examples cited could have been expanded into illustrations.

Illustrations may be especially valuable if they come from the speaker's own experience. In making his point that the Statue of Liberty is a symbol of hope, Lee Iacocca related:

Last fall I met a Vietnamese artist—one of the boat people who've taken such horrible risks to escape that country.

She settled in Alaska and came all the way down to Seattle to present me with a beautiful painting in honor of the Statue of Liberty. She still had some trouble with the language, but she had no trouble at all communicating how much America meant to her. (Iacocca 1985, 346)

The Analogy

An excellent way to make a claim clear is to make it analogous with something the audience already knows. Analogy is sometimes called the poorest form of argument because to make a logical case, the two things being compared must be alike in all respects except for the unknown feature the speaker needs to explain. Analogies seldom pass such a strict test of logic, but their power to explain remains unimpaired.

Tower used two analogies in quick succession. As he ended his claim that excessive regulation was costly, he said, "It doesn't take an economic expert to understand that the U.S. economy is under severe strain. Our daily headlines read like the hospital chart of a very sick patient—all the vital signs are moving in the wrong direction." This analogy stresses the magnitude in the cost claim, and it serves as a transition to the next claim, that the range of forces involved in regulation are numerous. Perhaps recognizing that an analogy serves clarity more than believability, Tower said, "I don't want to exaggerate, but it's like sensing the distant hoofbeats of the Four Horsemen of the Apocalypse."

At times an analogy may be reduced to little more than a figure of speech as in the "domino theory," the "lame duck politician," or a "level playing field in government regulation." Speakers with an ear for a vivid phrase, such as Colorado's governor, Richard Lamm, make good use of short analogies. Speaking on the immigration problem, Lamm began one address with an analogy in calling for the United States to "change course" in its immigration policy. In pointing to failures of the present policy, he used two additional analogies in a mixed metaphor to emphasize his argument: "As every house needs a door, so every country needs a border. And yet our borders are a virtual sieve" (Lamm 1985, 6).

Statistics

In spite of the negative attitude some people have toward statistics, numbers can be useful in proving a point. Statistics can be made interesting as well as logical and should be used with a positive tone. Writers who start with the apologetic, "I don't want to bore you with statistics, but . . ." will put any speaker at a disadvantage.

Statistics will be more meaningful if they are rounded off and put in context (although there will be times when precise figures must be cited). Almost no one in an audience will absorb the figure "$4,879,362.27," but "nearly five million dollars" might stick. Writing "4.7 percent" (which the speaker will read as the deadly dull "four-point-seven percent") is not as good as "about 5 percent," which is not as good as "about one out of twenty." Claiming that a company physical fitness program is affordable, Brenda Simonson replaced numbers altogether: "To put this in perspective: The cost of the average size Christmas party for employees could equip and staff a modest wellness center for a year" (Simonson 1986, 568).

In another case, a speaker took some mind-numbing numbers and made sense of them. Barrie L. Jones, vice-president of Howard Chase, made the claim that public relations professionals need to understand scale to do their jobs well. He supported that claim with statistics:

Let me give you an example of scale in our own turf. I collected press releases reporting third quarter earnings from ten of the major oil companies. These announcements were made during the week of October 22-31. Let's take the Phillips 66 press release to illustrate the value of scale. Now, why don't you take out a pencil and a piece of paper. I need your help with some math. Please write down these figures. In its third quarter, Phillips 66 reported revenues of $2,555,000,000. In round numbers, its earnings for the quarter were $190,000,000. Now, take your pencil and eliminate the last three digits in both revenues and earnings. That gives us revenues of $2,500,000 and earnings of $190,000. Got your pencils ready? O.K., let's cross out the last three digits again. Now, Phillips' revenues are $2,500 and its earnings are $190. Isn't this fun? Let's do it again. But this time just knock out one digit from both revenues and earnings. Now we have revenues of $250 and earnings of $19. My experience in financial matters is nowhere near the level of competence represented in this room. But can anyone of you tell me that the severest critics will find earnings of $19 on revenues of $250 an unacceptably high return? (Jones 1980, 217)

J. Peter Grace has answered the question, "What is a trillion?" in this way:

Now we all know that a billion is a million million and a trillion is a thousand billion, that's easy. But we put it in Volkswagens or Novas, we put it in six-packs, you name it, and we couldn't really envision a trillion. Then we did it in time. If somebody was born when Jesus Christ was born and had lived all this time and started counting seconds "1 . . . 2. . . 3 . . . 4," he'd be up to 62.5 billion right now, which is 6¼ percent of a trillion. It takes 31,700 years to count a trillion seconds. Now that's 317 centuries and we're in the 20th. (Grace 1985, 419)

A speech writer's sense of logic, along with the critical readings a speech gets in the approval process, should be enough to make sure statistics are fair and accurate. The writer's biggest job is to make them clear and interesting.

Quotations

A quotation can help make a claim understandable and believable in two ways. First, it may state the idea well. Some speakers who would not dare be caught in public with an eloquent phrase of their own will allow a well-worded idea to appear if it is a quotation. Second, a quotation can bring to bear the testimony of an expert to supplement the authority of the speaker.

Often a quotation can combine these two virtues. John Hanley used such a quotation in support of a claim that the controlled use of chemicals should be allowed in food production:

The respected nutritionist, Dr. Jean Mayer, has said that the public must try to "distinguish between real problems, unsupported claims, and the mouthings of food cranks. Otherwise," Dr. Mayer says, "there may soon be a national tendency to eat nothing but bean sprouts and alfalfa, on which a few deluded souls have already undertaken to survive." (Hanley 1977, 628)

Prime Minister Margaret Thatcher used both features of the quotation in supporting her strong stand in foreign policy in an address before the U.S. Congress. Military defense deters an enemy, she said, in citing Bismarck's phrase, "Do I want war? Of course not, I want victory" (Thatcher 1985, 323).

Speech writers should not scatter quotations through a speech with wild abandon. Although there can be no firm rule, three or four quotations in a fifteen- to twenty-minute speech do not seem excessive. Using ten or more almost certainly would cross the boundary.

Quotations should be kept short. Paraphrase all but the "good parts" or, as Hanley does, break the quotation up. A long quotation will challenge the delivery skills of the best speakers, and the worst ones will put their audiences to sleep.

Avoid writing the words *quote* and *end quote*. They sound strange. If the speaker's voice does not signal the end of the quotation, tell the audience the quotation is over by writing a tag line such as, "I believe Mr. Expert's words offer sound advice," or write in a transition to the next idea. Most of the time a pause or a change in tone will be enough, and often the precise ending point of the quote does not matter anyway.

No writer should invent quotations and in fact should take great care to make sure of the accuracy of a quotation before using it. A writer should also be realistic about what a speaker can reasonably expect to have read. Quotations culled from collections can make a speaker look foolish. In one case, a person doing research for a speech took Brutus's line, "There is a tide in the affairs of men . . ." from a book of quotations and in his notes recorded only the play as the source. Having no knowledge at all of Shakespeare, the speaker then stood before a college audience and read, "As Julius Caesar once said . . ."

Additional Forms of Support

Although examples, illustration, analogy, statistics, and quotations are the primary means of supporting a claim, a few additional types are worth noting. Explanation can be used to support a point. The speaker says, "What I mean is . . ." to fix a claim in listeners' minds without actually bringing any evidence to bear on the point. Restatement and repetition may be used. Martin Luther King, Jr.'s "I have a dream" statement made his point stronger with each repetition. Descriptions, definitions, and even mild expletives ("Now, how about that!") could help build a claim.

The five main types of support, however, remain the basic evidence on which a claim will stand or fall. As an interesting experiment, a writer might go through the body of a speech manuscript, carefully drawing lines through the five kinds of evidence. The object of the experiment would be to see how much was left unmarked. In theory at least, the only unmarked lines would be the claims plus any language used for such purposes as summary or transition. If a great deal is left unmarked, the manuscript is probably a mass of claims supported by other claims with no solid evidence to help an audience understand or believe.

TYPES OF PROOF

Early in the history of the study of public speaking, the classical rhetoricians asked a question of fundamental importance: what causes a listener to accept a speaker's ideas? Gradually the theory emerged that all the kinds of evidence speakers use could be classified in one or more of three categories of proof: the logic of the argument, the emotions felt by the audience, and the person of the speaker. The three kinds of proof were accepted as the forces that caused listeners to believe or act. A given piece of evidence in a speech, then, can build a logical case for the claim, create an emotional response favorable to the claim, or bring out qualities of the speaker that might influence the listener to accept the claim. Although the classical division of proof may not be a fully adequate explanation of human behavior (to a behaviorist of the B. F. Skinner school, for example), it provides a roughly accurate guide to the forces that guide many of our daily activities.

Are we influenced sometimes by logic? The answer is yes for anyone in the market for a lawn mower who first went to a consumer magazine for a methodical study of the most reasonable choice. (A small role might be played by the desire to get the best bargain.)

Are we influenced sometimes by emotion? The answer is yes for any suburbanite who has replaced a battered and ugly but serviceable automobile to avoid the shame of being outclassed by the shiny new model next door.

Are we influenced sometimes by the person of a persuader? The answer is yes for the homeowner who buys a lawn mower from a friend who owns a hardware store instead of buying a cheaper or higher-quality model from a stranger.

At a practical level, then, the categories are useful. A speech writer should make sure that a speech contains evidence from all three categories.

Logical Proof

Logical proof can be said to consist of supplying enough examples, illustrations, analogies, statistics, and/or quotations to satisfy the audience that the claim advanced is reasonable. The process involves both quality and quantity.

The quality of the evidence depends on its accuracy and its relevance to the claim being made. Once the accuracy of data is verified, a writer can establish relevance only if the claim has been clearly isolated. To be logical, the evidence must intelligently reinforce the claim. If a speaker makes the claim, "It was wrong to forbid prayer in public schools," and supports the claim by citing the rise in the number of students enrolling in private schools, there is little doubt of the accuracy of the evidence. But the evidence clearly fails the test of relevance. It does not support the claim.

The quantity of evidence needed may be harder to determine. How much is enough? A single example may prove a point in some cases. In another instance, a dozen pieces of evidence drawn from all five of the types may barely do the job. The writer must decide.

Emotion

Recognizing that listeners are moved by their emotions does not mean that the speech or the speaker should be emotional. Rather, it means that emotions of the audience must be taken into account in choosing material to back up claims.

Appeals to the emotions are common in everyday communication. We find them in advertising and in normal conversational exchanges at home or at work. A speech on almost any controversial topic will be delivered to an audience that has already had its emotions appealed to by persuaders on the other side of the argument.

In any society, most people are motivated by the same basic emotional drives. The following list includes some but not all the emotions that impel a typical modern Western audience: fear, greed, love, friendship, independence, conformity, fair play, patriotism, sympathy, security, and recognition. President Reagan's Martin Treptow illustration appealed strongly to patriotism and sympathy. Barrie L. Jones's statistics on Phillips 66 return compared to revenue appealed to fair play. Raymond Tower appealed to greed in telling business executives of the cost of regulation (although other appeals were also present), and he appealed to fear in warning of the huge number of regulators and their supporters. Even when attacking the emotionalism of supporters of regulation with his illustration of the story from *National Geographic*, Tower used emotion in appealing to fair play.

Lee Iacocca's story of the Vietnamese artist made a moving appeal to patriotism. His speech also appealed to both local and national pride in another way; the talk was delivered before the Poor Richard Club of Philadelphia, and Iacocca mentioned Ben Franklin by name more than twenty-five times (Iacocca 1985, 342-46). Although emotional proof should be used deliberately, a speech writer does not ordinarily go out with a shopping list of emotional appeals and systematically gather a bagful to put in a speech. In the normal course of writing a speech, they will usually appear. Knowledge of the specifics of motive appeals helps the speech writer primarily in the editing process.

It is often useful to read a manuscript through for a single purpose. One reading might be devoted exclusively to checking the use of emotional appeals (and another could be limited to checking organization or to reading only for vividness of language). In editing for emotional appeals, a writer should first make sure the speech has not been made purely logical with no concern for audience feeling. Then the variety of appeals should be studied. A writer may easily slip into the habit of relying excessively on one or two appeals—fear and greed, for example. Part of the concern in checking for variety is to make sure some nobler appeals are included. Finally, motives should not be dictated. President Reagan did not say, "If we have any patriotism in our hearts, we must respect the sacrifice of Martin Treptow." The president simply told the story.

Person of the Speaker

A writer would be making a serious error to neglect the use of the speaker's character as a means of persuasion. When it is neglected, the reason seems to be the fear speakers and writers have that references to the speaker will appear egotistical. Add to that the drill many writers have had in avoiding the personal pronoun, and the obstacles to using the speaker's character may be formidable.

But speaking is a personal means of communication, and ego is less a function of what is said than it is of that mysterious force we call personality. People who are egotistical reveal their ego in manner more than in ideas. They show their ego in style and tone. An egotistical person might speak egotistically of the weather, while a modest person can speak of great accomplishments modestly. As Dizzy Dean is supposed to have said, "If you done it, it ain't braggin'."

The speaker's character can appear in a speech by showing the speaker's knowledge, concern and integrity. These useful aspects of personal proof may be referred to as "I know," "I care," and "I am not a crook." This type of proof appears most often in the openings and conclusions of speeches; it serves a good purpose there, but it should be used as well throughout the speech in support of a speaker's claims.

"*I know.*" Indicating a speaker's personal knowledge of the subject of a speech involves two steps. First, examples, illustrations, statistics, analogies, and quotations should be based where possible on the speaker's experience. Second, the speaker's first-hand acquaintance with the material should be made clear to the audience. "I saw," "I read," "I recall," and "I went" are simple phrases that can turn a routine piece of evidence into impressive support for a claim. "The latest figures reveal" can often be replaced with "I studied with care the facts we recently collected."

Former Postmaster General William Bolger gave a dramatic touch to an otherwise routine quotation in support of his claim that public attitude affects inflation: "To quote a young woman I heard interviewed recently, 'Why should I care if the price of a "Big Mac" goes from $1.69 to $1.99 or whatever, as long as my wages go up, too'" (Bolger 1980, 241).

To illustrate his point that supervision is important, Timken Company president Joseph Toot said:

To put this thesis in sharp focus for all of us, permit me to use as a vehicle an incident that occurred at one of my company's bearing manufacturing plants several months ago. This example may not be an especially dramatic one, but I would submit that it illustrates quite well the kinds of things than can fall apart when there is a failure of supervision. An operator in the plant to which I refer was responsible for running two screw machines. (Toot 1980, 237) [In order to call attention to the fact that illustrations hold interest through curiosity, as was pointed out in the previous chapter, this story will be left unfinished.]

At times a writer can recognize instances where the speaker's personal experience would be especially important. This appears to be the case when, in addressing the delicate issue of homosexuality and AIDS, Melvin Anchell illustrated his knowledge as follows:

During the past 15 years, I have been called upon, from time to time, to appear as an expert witness in psychiatry and human sexuality. My testimony in these court cases has been as a witness for the local, state and Federal governments. Recently, I was called to Washington as an advisor to the Office for Families which is a part of HHS [Department of Health and Human Services].

Forty years of medical experience in psychiatry and general medicine, have taught me that homosexuality . . . (Anchell 1986, 286)

"I Care." Statements of concern are powerful when they are sincere. They appear in daily conversation, and they can be added easily to speeches. In almost any speech manuscript written in an impersonal style, three or four paragraphs can usually be found where it would be quite natural to add a line. Assuming the statement to be true, it would simply say, "And I want you to know I am deeply concerned about this matter" or "We here at Ajax are determined to keep our service at this high level." After a brief discussion of his plans to attend a summit meeting, President Reagan in an address to the country added, "This, then, is why I go to Geneva: To build a foundation for lasting peace" (Reagan 1985, 98).

Here are some examples of expressed concern from a single issue of *Vital Speeches:*

I know that what I'm saying isn't the popular thing to say. But I am convinced it must be done. (Bolger 1980, 242)

Let me make it clear, I do not question the good intentions of all the vast army of men and women who operate the agencies and bureaus that spend billions of our tax dollars. (Gould 1980, 235)

I'm not saying that everything will be business as usual. It won't. But I don't find that bad—I find it invigorating. (Ostar 1980, 243)

But I do not despair. I think there will be tremendous opportunities in the '80s and '90s. I believe we can and will overcome many of our current problems. (Buckley 1980, 251)

"I Am Not a Crook." Demonstrating a speaker's integrity presents a writer with a delicate problem. Queen Gertrude's terse, "The lady doth protest too much," reminds us of the dangers of a too ostentatious show of honor. But occasions arise when a direct statement of the speaker's honesty should be made.

Former Postmaster General Bolger established his candor indirectly in his defense of the efficiency of the mails: "Individual lapses will, and do, occur; they always have. But I think any fairminded person would allow this is inevitable when we are dealing with the daily movement of 300 million items" (Bolger 1980, 241).

And John Caldwell, international vice-president of the U.S. Chamber of Commerce, hastened to spell out his moral stand after making an attack on what he considered to be a selective application of a human rights policy: "It is also interesting to note that human rights violations committed by Israel seem to enjoy far less publicity in our press than petty features of South Africa's policy of apartheid—which, incidentally, I do not condone either" (Caldwell 1980, 252).

COMPLEXITY OF EVIDENCE AND PROOF

At no point in this discussion is it implied that the types of evidence and the categories of proof are neatly compartmentalized in the actual presentation of a speech. An illustration may include statistics, and a quotation may contain an analogy. A logical example may appeal to fear, and a statement of concern may evoke a strong feeling of patriotism in an audience. Listeners are not targets in a shooting gallery with so many points awarded for a logical statistic and so many points for an emotional example. But the ability to identify elements of proof and types of evidence gives a writer a system for evaluating a speech. An appreciation of the classical approach to proof, like an understanding of good organization, should be creative. Comprehending the relationship between claims and support ought to broaden a writer's options while helping produce sound speeches.

COUNTERARGUMENTS

At times a writer knows an audience will be aware of arguments against the position being taken in a speech, or perhaps the counterarguments soon will be made public. In such a case, it is better to get the counterarguments out into the open.

Research conducted over the past thirty years suggests that intelligent and well-informed audiences will be more easily convinced if they hear both sides in a controversy. They are also more likely to stay convinced longer if they hear both points of view while making up their minds.

These results square with common sense. A speaker confident and candid enough to bring out opposing arguments exerts a strong appeal, and the counterarguments an audiences hears later from another source will have lost some of their power to dissuade because they have already been taken into account.

A writer can choose from among three basic strategies: the counterargument can be granted, balanced, or refuted.

Grant the Counterargument

Few corporate executives or government officials like to come right out and say good arguments can be made against positions they take. But such a course may be sound. Owen Butler, chairman of the Board of Procter and Gamble, thought so in defending Procter and Gamble's sponsorship of television programs under attack for excessive sex and violence (Butler 1981, 522). Butler made the claim in his speech that Procter and Gamble remained "perfectly willing to defend" the show "White Shadow" in spite of certain controversial espiodes. Then he conceded a point to his critics: "What we can't defend is the pre-show publicity which included ads placed without our knowledge and featuring the headline 'Teacher Seduces Student.'" Although Butler's immediate audience was made up of professional television people, his granting of an argument that had been published in a Federation of Decency newsletter was no doubt aimed in part at a distant audience.

Another example may be seen in a speech delivered by a U.S. military officer at a historically black university. The address developed a theme of black progress in the armed services. The audience responded well, and the speech won support for the military. The text of the address, however, offered many instances of the failure of the military to do a better job of giving equal treatment, and the speech ignored many recent improvements. This approach might seem backward at first, but it bears out research findings suggesting at times granting the correctness of opposition arguments may be the best way to handle them. Had the military speaker devoted his time to a rosy account of progress, many listeners would have blocked out his message while thinking about the counterarguments.

Granting a counterargument does not mean the speaker has to grovel. In fact, it is usually a good idea to avoid words such as *concede* and *admit*. The speaker can "recognize" or "realize" or "be aware of" counterarguments without appearing weak. Speaking out forcefully for the union movement, a former AFL-CIO officer realized that many in his industrial relations audience had vivid memories of the strike of the air traffic controllers. "PATCO should not have struck," he said. "The whole labor movement lost with the loss of PATCO" (Perlis 1984, 733).

Balancing Counterarguments

A writer may deal with opposition points by bringing them up and balancing them off with points on the speaker's side of the issue. This method still means granting the negative point, but it does not stop there. An example of how this method can be used appears in the Bolger statement cited above that in handling the mail, "individual lapses do occur," but the postal service deals with "the daily movement of 300 million items."

In preparing to defend U.S. business across a broad front, GE's Reginald Jones first conceded,

There are plenty of reasons for concern.

Just look at the headlines. E. F. Hutton kiting checks. Runs on banks in Ohio, Maryland and elsewhere. So far this year, 80 banks have failed—more than in any year since the Great Depression. Prominent bankers and financiers behind bars—and this is the staid old banking business.

Or consider the impact of the daily news stories about take-over battles. "Greenmail!" "Poison pills!" "Junk bonds!" "Golden parachutes!" What does the public think of the corporate raiders, out to make a bundle not by offering new products or services, but simply through financial manipulation? (Jones 1985, 253).

Refuting Counterarguments

The third approach to counterarguments, and perhaps the most common except for ignoring them, calls for the writer to show they are wrong. In the aftermath of the Love Canal controversy, the president of Hooker Chemical, Donald L. Baeder, took on the arguments against his company and his industry. His defense was bold. Apparent concessions to opposition arguments turn out not to be concessions after all: "First, we *do* have a problem . . . but it is not the problem that is commonly perceived" and "Candidly, we in the chemical industry must share part of the blame for public skepticism . . . because we generally did not do enough to explain our efforts to the public" (Baeder 1980, 496-500). Baeder attacked charges of past industry irresponsibility head-on. Using analogies with changes that have occurred in scientific understanding of dealing with X-rays and asbestos, he built a case that the chemical industry should not be judged "using today's standards applied to *past* practices or for not knowing what was *unknowable* at the time."

Another example of direct refutation of counterarguments can be found in the combative address, "What's So Wrong with 'The Military Industrial Complex?'" delivered by General James Mullins. Taking on the issue of defense costs, he said,

It's also important for Americans to understand that defense represents only 17 percent of our total public spending, which is down from a post war high of 36 percent in 1955. In fact, today it represents only about 6 percent of our Gross National Product—less than half what the Soviets spend—and about 17 percent of what we spent during the height of World War II. (Mullins 1983, 134)

CONCLUSION

Aristotle concluded that the essence of the art of speaking was to discover in each individual case all the means of persuasion available to the speaker.

At the heart of that process is the determination of the claims to be made and the material at hand to support those claims. Identifying claims and supporting them adequately can be difficult and even tedious, but it is necessary for the writer who wants a speech to be more than a string of glittering generalities.

6

Writing in an Oral Style

I am by calling a dealer in words, and words are, of course, the most powerful drug used by mankind.

—Rudyard Kipling

Words make a difference. Those who claim the idea is everything—and such people seem to come rather often from the ranks of the scientific and technically minded—see only half the communications formula. Words without ideas will never amount to much, but ideas need to be articulated well to have an impact.

The writer works with but two variables: word choice and word combination. The whole matter of style boils down to choosing one word over another and then selecting the best possible combination of words.

When a U.S. general said "Nuts" in answer to a Nazi surrender demand in World War II, he chose the right word to make his message last. When John F. Kennedy strung together the words *ask, not, what, your, country, can, do, for, you,* he selected ordinary words but cast then in an order that made his phrase one of the most quoted passages in modern public speaking. Churchill demonstrated the mastery of word choice and word combination in such phrases as "blood, tears, toil, and sweat."

Can the manipulation of the variables be learned by someone wishing to improve? Teaching style always works better after the fact. That is, anyone who wishes to teach the effective use of language can do a far better job of singling out good examples than straightening out bad habits. Columnist

James J. Kilpatrick takes a pessimistic view in his statement, "None of us can explain what is meant by style and none of us can tell someone else how to go about acquiring style" (Kilpatrick 1981, A8).

Although it is far easier to learn new patterns of organization or fresh ways to use evidence than it is to change language habits, three areas of study can help writers produce better speeches: study of the distinctive features of oral language as opposed to language to be read silently, a review of selected basics that apply to all good writing but have a particular value in writing speeches, and consideration of the rhetorical devices that effective speakers seem to use so often.

ORAL LANGUAGE

We do not use the same language to express an idea in speaking that we use in writing. As a well-known professor of public speaking once put it, "A speech is not an essay standing on its hind legs." A great British orator, Charles James Fox, insisted that a speech that read well in the newspaper was sure to have been a bad speech. And lawyer Louis Nizer noted that "even great writers and poets who are experts in molding words are often helpless in the realm of speaking. Public speaking must be recognized as a separate art. . . . The words may be the same, but the grammar, rhetoric and parsing are different. It is a different mode of expression—a different language" (Nizer 1944, 22).

Our educational system allows few opportunities to put speaking language down on paper. Much formal training in writing actually discourages any effort to capture the language of speech on the printed page. Speech writers with an established record of successful business, journalistic, or academic writing may find they have to break old habits.

One quite simple device will catch most of the words and phrases in a speech that strike the ear as wrong. The writer should read the speech into a tape recorder. Some changes can be made on the basis of how the words feel as they are read. When the tape is played back, a few more awkward spots can be fixed.

By reading and hearing the speech in draft form and by remembering a few of the characteristics of oral language, a writer should be able to produce a manuscript that captures the flavor of speech. It is important to remember that only the flavor of conversational speech is desired. Good language for a manuscript speech is not exactly the same as that of normal conversation. Cleaned up and taken out of the manuscript will be vocalizations such as "and," "ah," or "er." Also missing for the most part will be a number of what we might call nonwords sprinkled through much conversation in the form of "mmmmmm," "huh?" and "hah." Much of the twisted syntax present when a speaker gropes for a thought will be missing too.

Wordiness

Writers have generally been taught to regard conciseness as a virtue in style. But as the eighteenth-century rhetorician Hugh Blair pointed out:

Discourses that are to be spoken require a more copious style than books that are to be read. When the whole meaning must be catched from the mouth of the speaker, without the advantage which books afford of pausing at pleasure and reviewing what appears obscure, great conciseness is always to be avoided. (Blair 1793, 2: 13-14)

The injunction to write concisely has its roots in the principle that no more words should be used than are necessary to communicate a thought. That principle holds for speech as well as writing, but it must be applied differently. In part because of the instantaneous nature of communication in speaking, most ideas require more words to be understood in speaking than would be needed in silent reading. The objective, however, remains the same in speech as in reading: to use no more than the number of words needed to communicate successfully.

Speakers add words in an effort to get their ideas across in three ways: they repeat ideas, they stretch out ideas, and they pile on more evidence than they would use in most writing.

Repetition. Writers for the eye as well as writers for the ear may find it useful to repeat. In the Declaration of Independence, Thomas Jefferson, by no means an orator, leveled seventeen consecutive charges against King George, all beginning with the phrase *he has.* He wrote seven clauses in a row starting with the word *for,* and in the span of four sentences he included four *we have's* and one *nor have we.*

The Declaration, however, was a distinctly oratorical piece of writing, and repetition is not as common in print as it is in such passages as "I have a dream" from Martin Luther King, Jr., or Churchill's "We shall fight on the beaches. We shall fight on the landing grounds. We shall fight in the fields and in the streets, and we shall fight in the hills."

In a commencement speech, Boston University president John Silber quoted part of the argument from Biff and Willy Loman from *Death of a Salesman.* Then he said:

We do not have to choose between Biff and Willy. Both are right. They are a dime a dozen, and they are magnificent. The fact about human beings is that we are both a dime a dozen and we are magnificent. If we only believe we are magnificent, we become insufferably arrogant at best. . . . On the other hand if we believe we are merely a dime a dozen, we lose our reason for being. (Silber 1986, 593).

Silber closed the speech with the two lines: "Of course we are all a dime a dozen. And we are all magnificent."

Stretching Out. "Nuts" was a rhetorically satisfactory answer for

General McAuliffe to give the Nazis, but in an oral style, a sentence may be stretched out even to the point of redundancy. For example, a sign saying "tow-away zone" presents all the basic information a driver needs to learn a particular piece of information. But the owner of a café in a small Texas town produced a much more conversational version: "No Parking. Violators Will Be Towed Away at Owner's Expense." The word *away* is clearly redundant, and the claim that violators will be towed (rather than vehicles) is inaccurate. We might assume that the author of the sign would fare better as a speech writer than as a newspaper editor.

In a speech discussing a series of periods of history, an early draft contained the phrase "from 1946 to 1969." To help the audience absorb the idea—and to help separate more emphatically this period of time from others in the speech—the phrase was stretched in a later draft. It then read, "During the more than twenty years from the end of World War II to the close of the 1960s." The second version has three times as many words as the first, it gives the number of years as well as the time span contained in the first draft, and it uses extra words to give landmarks at the beginning and the end of the period in question.

Adding Evidence. A writer may choose to support a claim in a written report with as large a volume of evidence as would be used in a speech, but often the written claim will require far less support. A limited amount of evidence can be submitted on the assumption that the reader can absorb the full impact of whatever is presented. A listener, on the other hand, might be expected to need a greater quantity of evidence because the words go by so quickly.

Marilyn Loden, speaking on networking, indicates how speakers often pile up evidence to make a point:

Working women are deluged today with recipes for success. Walk into any bookstore and you'll find a dozen books loaded with advice for the working woman on "how to dress for success," how to become more assertive, how to learn the corporate "games mother never taught you," how to prepare gourmet meals in 10 minutes. I could go on all night with these "how to's." (Loden 1981, 614)

Because an idea takes more words to develop in speaking than it does in writing, a speech writer should make special efforts to limit the scope of a speech. A speaker may want to take on too broad a subject. Often a topic can be cut in half or even slashed to a third of its original scope. The remainder could then be made into a much better talk than would be possible with the broader subject.

Informal Word Choice

A speaker once referred to the laser as an invention that has the scientific world "agog." The audience was probably agog for a minute or two at hearing a word seldom spoken in informal speaking. In a speech to company employees, a high-ranking corporate officer began to discuss fringe benefits by saying "as you contemplate retirement . . ." The efforts the company was making to show concern for its employees was no doubt dampened somewhat by the word *contemplate*—a perfectly decent word in print that sounded stiff and formal in a speech that was supposed to be warm and caring.

The little word *for* has no place in a speech if used in the sense of "because." It looks fine, but it sounds out of place, as columnist Andy Rooney pointed out in criticizing many political speech writers. He suggested that they "are not used to writing words to be spoken aloud by someone else. Some of the speeches might look good on paper, but they sound terrible when they're spoken because they are contrived and unnatural." As an example he cited, "*for* our nation must always remember" and "We must match our concern with action, *for* without such action." Rooney noted, "Almost no one but politicians uses 'for' in that sense as a conjunction, and it sounds pompous. 'Because' would almost always be better" (Rooney 1980, A8).

Many words ending in -*ly* strike the ear as too formal: *firstly* for *first*, *importantly* for *important*, or *alternatively* for the phrase *as an alternative*. Starting sentences with -*ing* words often sounds odd, as in the sentence, "Being hungry, we stopped to eat."

Words that refer to physical locations in a manuscript, commonly used in writing, should be avoided in speeches. *Above* and *below* are good examples. Even *following* and *preceding* refer as much to space as to time and should rarely be used.

The list could be expanded. Usually *on* sounds better than *upon*, *also* better than *moreover*, *find out* better than *ascertain*, *use* better than *utilize*, and *that* better than *which*. Words with an archaic ring (*whence, hence, thus, whereupon*) generally should be replaced. Of course, in quotations or in an deliberate effort to achieve formality, some of the formal language of writing can be effective. No suggestion about style can be firm without knowing the context in which the language appears.

Nothing has been said here about jargon. Jargon represents a problem not of formality but of clarity and will be discussed later. Understanding the speaker is not the point now being raised. All of the words criticized so far make perfectly good sense to a normal person. The employees understood *contemplate*, but the word destroyed the desired tone of the message.

Some authorities claim speaking uses shorter words than writing. But as the examples demonstrate, that rule does not always apply. A speech writer needs "talking words," no matter how long they are.

Rhythm

Although a speech should not have the firm cadence of "The Charge of the Light Brigade," rhythm is slightly more important in spoken than in written prose. Occasionally a sentence in print jars a reader because the beat is off, but the harm is not as great as in the case of speaking.

One writer's sense of rhythm may not be the same as that of another writer. The simplest way to judge cadence is to depend on the ear. The following sentence has a flaw in its rhythm: "He marched through corporate America leaving a trail behind him of profit and growth." Reading it aloud should suggest a change. One solution is to invert two pairs of words to produce, "He marched through corporate America leaving behind him a trail of profit and growth." Now the sentence flows in the manner of normal speech.

Rhythm takes on greater importance in speaking than in writing because of the element of time. Most readers pick up phrases and even sentences all at once, but the listener must get information one sound at a time. If a key word appears too early in a sentence, the listener may start to applaud or laugh while the speaker continues.

Climax. A writer will usually want to punch up a thought by making it the climax of a sentence or a paragraph. Rhythm, including the proper use of the pause, can create the climax. The sentence used as an illustration above could be changed to read, "He marched through corporate America leaving behind him a trail of profit—and of growth."

Climax often depends in part on the increasing importance of the ideas being expressed. A speech by Under Secretary of the Navy James Woolsey illustrates that approach in a passage with excellent rhythm: "The least desirable way to achieve victory is to destroy an enemy's cities; the next least desirable is to kill his soldiers; better is to destroy his alliances; but best of all is to destroy his plans and never have to fight at all" (Woolsey 1978, 568). This sentence combines climactic order with a conversational tone.

Clauses. Speech writers should avoid clauses. They should write sentences in a straightforward subject, verb, object order. Clauses ask a listener to hold in mind the idea in the first part of the sentence while a new or qualifying idea is injected. Readers can handle clauses; listeners have difficulty with them.

At times, clauses not only suspend an idea, they run the risk of insulting the audience. This will occur almost any time a clause is used to insert a person's qualifications. For example, if a speaker says, "Will Rogers, the famous humorist from Oklahoma, once said . . ." the audience is told, in effect, "Will Rogers, and since you don't know who he is, I'll tell you . . ." The qualification could be dropped in some cases. When it cannot—in this case, when a few members of the audience may not know who Will Rogers was or when it is important for some reason to make sure everyone remembers he was from Oklahoma—then the clause must be removed without eliminating the information. The sentence could read, "That famous Oklahoma humorist Will Rogers once said . . ."

Clauses can also be removed when they qualify. "I once lived in

Alabama, a state deep in the heart of the American South, where . . ."
becomes "I once lived deep in the heart of the American South in the state
of Alabama where . . ." The revised phrase has a better rhythm. Also,
moving from the general to the specific case rather than the other way around
avoids offending listeners.

When a writer finds it appropriate to insert material in the middle of a
sentence, the insertion should be set off with dashes rather than with
commas. If an idea is important enough to interrupt a sentence, it should be
done with more emphasis than that suggested by the punctuation of an ordinary clause. Usually speakers will make a more abrupt pause at a dash than
at a comma, and they are more likely to change vocal inflection to emphasize material set off in this manner. Andrew Cecil's address, "Independence
and World Citizenship," presents examples of dashes:

The alternative—God save us—is to perish together.

Crimes against humanity—the atrocities of arrest without trial, torture, and concen-
tration camps—are not solved at these conferences. (Cecil 1980)

The Spoken Sentence

The sentence of impromptu conversation bears little resemblance to the
sentence of formal, written English. As in other aspects of style, the
sentence of a manuscript speech borrows from both the spoken and the
written form.

A spoken sentence can be quite long. Short units of thought connected by
and or *but* form a single grammatical string that can stretch for hundreds of
words. When such a construction is used, it is meaningless to argue that
long sentences are harder to understand than short sentences. The argument
may be correct for long complex sentences with many clauses, but spoken
sentences are generally free of clauses. A more accurate statement would be
that long thought units are harder to understand than short thought units.
A page in this book could easily be filled with a sentence a speaker could
convey with little difficulty.

On paper, even in a speech manuscript, such a sentence would look
strange. But speech writers capture the essence of the long sentence flow by
putting periods before the conjunctions and starting many new sentences
with *and* or *but*. If the sentences express worthwhile ideas, writers should
not be deterred from starting them with conjunctions simply because of the
rules in some style book.

Speech writers should be more concerned with variety of length than with
keeping sentences short. A few one-word or two-word sentences can liven
up a talk. If all the sentences are kept at about the same length, the speech
will probably sound monotonous.

Personal Words

In the fine guide to style by William Strunk as revised by E. B. White, the first of the positive suggestions for improving writing calls for the writer to be kept in the background. The mood and temper of the writer should not be obvious in the language of good writing. However valuable this rule may be for the writer of reports and essays, it does not apply to the writer for spoken discourse. The personality of the speaker should emerge, and personal language will appear frequently in good speeches.

The use of personal proof demands personal language in a speech. So does the social nature of the speaking situation; speakers who never use the personal pronoun will appear too formal and distant for most public presentations. The speech writer faces the problem not of weeding out personal references but rather of finding ways to get them into a speech. The writer must know what the speaker can say with personal conviction and convince the speaker that such material should be in the manuscript.

Lee Iacocca's willingness—perhaps eagerness—to put himself into the language of his speeches helps account for his popularity on the public platform. In a speech to the Poor Richard Club, he said:

Of all the people in history, Ben Franklin is the man I'd most like to meet. I'd like to have a drink with him. (I'd have a scotch, and he'd have his glass of port.)

He'd probably start by saying, "Iacocca, that's a hell of a name. I never heard a name like that before." And I'd tell him all about the big wave of immigrants that came over. (I'd probably talk about that a lot because since I got involved with the Statue of Liberty and Ellis Island project, I've become something of an expert.)

I think he'd be pleased, for the most part. (Iacocca 1985, 343)

CHARACTERISTICS OF ALL GOOD LANGUAGE

Three characteristics of all good writing should guide speech writers in choosing and arranging words. The language of a speech should be clear, vivid, and appropriate.

Clarity

Making ideas clear starts with understanding how meaning is transferred in communication. Unfortunately, much schooling and practice in writing focuses on the correctness of language rather than on how words carry meaning. As a result, writers concentrate on the rules of grammar or the meaning in a dictionary. A better starting point for the speech writer would be a study of semantics: the study of how words mean.

Semantics explores the relationship between words and the concepts words convey. At the heart of this relationship is the realization that a word is but a symbol for an object or a concept in the speaker's mind. As the semanticists put it, "The word is not the thing."

The use of technical language illustrates the point. Technical experts are sometimes so concerned about the right word they forget that the word is but a symbol for the idea. Take the word *station*, for example, as it is used by engineers in the telephone industry. It means almost the same as *telephone*. But because there is a subtle difference between the two terms, many engineers resist the advice to use the almost correct *telephone*. The result is that most lay listeners are mystified by references to large numbers of *stations* in an engineer's speech. Like many other technical terms, *station* is so difficult to explain that the required explanation would seldom be worth the trouble. The almost correct term would do a far better job of making the engineer's idea clear to an audience.

Precise technical language has its role when one expert talks to another. Saying *telephone* instead of *station* could conceivably be a confusing and even costly mistake when one engineer communicates with another. The writer's concern, then, must be on how the symbol gets interpreted rather than on the so-called true meaning of a term.

The semantics approach to language suggests that meaning is found in people rather than in words. If the writer chooses a symbol that the listener associates with the concept in the speech, the language is clear. Clarity is not achieved simply because the writer and the speaker understand the words.

Even when a listener understands the words in a speech, the language will not clearly transmit the ideas of the speaker if the words distract. This may occur if sexist, racist, or other offending terms are used.

Sexist Language. Language considered sexist will call attention to the speaker's method of expression rather than to ideas. Such language may also cause some listeners to reach unflattering conclusions about the speaker's fairmindedness and about the degree to which the speaker shows sensitivity to social concerns.

The distractions of sexist language can easily be eliminated without creating another set of distractions based on clumsy, nonsexist terms. The expression *unmanned boat* might well deflect the attention of some listeners. But the nonsexist *unpeopled boat* would probably distract even more. Saying "a boat with no one on board" would solve the problem without calling attention to the solution.

Avoiding the generic *man*, eliminating terms such as *girls in the office,* and not applying *he*, *him*, or *his* to a person of unknown sex can accomplished by using a number of simple techniques.

Plural—The "he-his-him" problem can be readily solved by starting with a plural noun. Rather than saying, "Whenever he can, an employee should add to his credit union account," a writer can choose, "Whenever they can, employees should add to their credit union accounts." Using the plural will cause a slight loss of specificity, but if it is important in a particular case to make an example specific, a person can be named.

Hypothetical—if no actual case comes to mind, a hypothetical man or woman can be the subject of the example, which would then be specific without being sexist. The employee example used above, like many other examples, does not suffer from being made plural.

Repeat—The noun may be repeated to avoid the need for a pronoun. This approach cannot be used in every case, but it will sometimes work. For instance, "A doctor should remember that his first responsiblity is to . . ." can be replaced by, "A doctor should remember that a doctor's first responsibility is to . . ."

Substitute—The word *chairman* is hard to replace without calling attention to the change. Both *chair* and *chairperson* will be as offensive to some listeners as *chairman* is to others (and "chairperson of the board of Ajax Oil" just won't work). But most sexist terms can be readily replaced by terms that do not offend. *Businessman* becomes *business executive* or *person in business. Housewife* becomes *homemaker*. And *saleslady* becomes *salesperson*. In the case of unequal yoking found in the expression "man and wife," either of the terms may be substituted to produce "husband and wife" or "man and woman."

Cut—Often the offending word may be edited out of a manuscript. *Lady lawyer* can be reduced to *lawyer*, the *his* removed from "husband and his wife," and the *him* cut from "a citizen secure in the rights provided him by the Constitution."

And/Or—The examples cited so far have been designed to remove sexism without calling attention to the change. There may be times when a deliberate reference to both sexes will be in order. Reference may then be made to "a soldier beginning his or her duties," "a speaker addressing his or her audience," or "an executive solving his or her problems." Officers of the International Association of Business Communicators, an organization with a membership more than 50 percent female, sometimes refer to a member in the abstract as "she or he." The use of *or* plus the reversal of the more common order of the two words serves to emphasize a speaker's intent to recognize the actual makeup of the membership.

Objections to removing sexism from language often include ridiculous examples. *Personhole* for *manhole* or *woperson* for *woman* are sometimes cited as examples of changes needed to be consistent. If a writer remembers the semanticist's explanation of how meaning happens in communication, these examples are obviously absurd. The words *manhole* and *woman* in a proper context present almost no risk of offending anyone. The words *girl* in reference to adult females, *his* in reference to a person of unspecified gender, or *his wife* in the phrase "a man and his wife" do offend a significant number of people. Changing such expressions does less to make a political or social statement than it does to achieve clarity by directing attention to ideas and not to the words used to express the ideas.

Racist and Other Offending Terms. Just as sexist words distract, so may words that offend ethnic groups or words that are considered derogatory by increasing numbers of people who identify with disabled persons or older citizens. The word *black* should not be used in a negative sense but should be cut or replaced by any of several words that will carry the desired meaning without the possibility of embarrassment.

Public awareness of the offensive implications of such terms as *cripple*, *basket case*, *deaf and dumb*, and even *handicapped* has been relatively recent. Increasingly, more and more listeners in a wide variety of audiences will be sensitive to careless use of these words.

This discussion of words that distract is but an introduction to a complicated subject. The International Association of Business Communicators book, *Without Bias*, edited by Judy Pickens, and Miller and Swift's *The Handbook of Nonsexist Writing* explore the topics in more detail. The concern here has been limited to achieving clarity by avoiding distractions.

Vivid Language

Words have the ability to evoke all of the human senses. A vivid description of a headache in an aspirin commercial seems designed to make a viewer hurt, and any detailed conversational account of a broken arm will have the same effect on most listeners. A glowing account of a good meal does in fact make the mouth water; words can create an image almost real enough to appeal to the taste buds. The sense of smell and the sense of hearing are a bit harder to awaken with words, but any listener who has mowed a lawn or witnessed a thunderstorm may have the smells and sounds of those events brought back by a lively description of them in a speech.

The visual image is perhaps the most common and the most useful. A good description can transmit a picture to a listener's mind where it will stick. "The Iron Curtain" captures a concept so well with a picture that the phrase from a Churchill speech was added to the language of international politics. A business speaker fixed an image in the mind of an audience with equal success by reminding them that before the days of the automobile, pollution from transportation came in the form of horse manure on the streets.

A good image in a speech must be worded with sufficient detail to permit the audience to see the picture. Color, size, shape, movement, and direction are among the elements that can be included. Karl Eller, president of Combined Communications Corporation, used a vivid description of milk production to illustrate the free enterprise system:

I'm going to leave you with a little reminder. That reminder is a glass of milk. . . . But look at that milk and think about what it took to bring that glass of milk to your table. Some farmer bred and raised the cow. Some farmer owned and tended the land it grazed on. . . . Some farmer milked the cow or cows and sold the milk to someone else who processed it, pasteurized it and packaged it. . . . And all along the line the product was either made better or its distribution was simplified and narrowed and a lot of people had jobs. Wealth was created. Someone was paid to haul the milk to the restaurant and paid to carry it inside and put it in the refrigerator. The waitress was paid wages. . . . You ordered milk. You got milk. But you got more than milk. You got a miracle in a glass. The miracle of created wealth. (Eller 1979, 232)

Appropriate Language

In a speech, "The Last Best Hope: Words," Mel Grayson made the point that a writer must have more than one style. The writer in corporate communications, Grayson believes, needs "the whole gamut of words and sentence structures—the involved and complex as well as the bare-bones simple" (Grayson 1981, 588).

Speech writers need the ability to switch styles as required not only from the company newsletter to a speech manuscript but also from one company speaker to another and from one speaking occasion to another. A passage composed for one speech may crop up in a later talk on the same general subject. Writers in an organization freely borrow from one another, so a section of one speech may be transferred to a talk by another speaker. A politician on a hectic schedule may deliver essentially the same message to several audiences. In each instance, fine tuning of the language will often be required. It must be appropriate for each speaker, each audience, and each occasion. Russell Conwell delivered his lecture, "Acres of Diamonds," over five thousand times, but he adjusted it slightly for each audience.

President Franklin Roosevelt had an especially good ear for the right word on the right occasion. When Frances Perkins wrote for him, she included in a social security speech the line, "We are trying to construct a more inclusive society." When she heard the speech on her car radio, Roosevelt had changed the passage to read, "We are going to make a country in which no one is left out."

Although each speech does not have to be completely new, it must be adapted to fit the needs of the new situation. Any suggestion made in the discussion of language in this chapter should be ignored if it would cause a writer to violate the rule of appropriateness.

RHETORICAL DEVICES

Speakers manipulate language in some ways that cannot properly be classified as oral style. Although the same devices are sometimes found in writing, this use of language appears to have particular value in front of an audience.

Fragments

Speech writers may add variety to a talk by including an occasional sentence fragment. Ronald Reagan's First Inaugural Address had several incomplete sentences in it. The following example has two in just one paragraph: "Professionals, industrialists, shopkeepers, clerks, cabbies and truck drivers. They are, in short, 'We the people.' This breed called Americans."

The sentence fragment in a manuscript looks somewhat more like a deliberate rhetorical device than a reflection of normal speech patterns. That appears to be true in the Reagan example. But fragments do occur at times in normal speech: "No way." "Lots of luck." "A hundred dollars!" "Wonderful, wonderful, wonderful."

Rhetorical Questions

Like the sentence fragment, the rhetorical question adds variety to the language of a speech. It has two additional virtues. First, it helps bridge the gap between the speaker and the audience. A question attempts to break through to the audience, to engage listeners' minds. Second, the rhetorical question adds a dramatic note. An issue is phrased in a compelling way; questions imply mystery and perhaps even a sense of urgency. A question can forcefully draw attention to a speaker's point: "What can we do, then, to restore the vitality of American industry? I say we must redouble our efforts in research and development."

The dramatic effect of a rhetorical question may be enhanced by presenting it as coming from someone else: "Our critics ask" or "The responsible buyer must wonder how we are able. . . ."

Rhetorical questions have an even greater impact when several are used together. In arguing that corporations should give 5 percent of their profits to charity, Kenneth N. Dayton grouped three questions. Phrasing his questions as though they came from the audience, he said, "At this point you might ask, 'Why five percent?' Why strive for the maximum? Why not go along with the national average of about one percent?" At another point Dayton clustered three questions to stress the benefits of corporate contributions: "How many Lyric Theatres would that build? How much Cancer research would that fund? How many Hispanic programs?" (Dayton 1980, 619-22).

Although rhetorical questions are usually phrased to elicit an affirmative answer, they may be designed to stress the negative. On the theory that an audience may be stronger in its opposition to what it dislikes than in support for what it likes, writers may find this approach useful. Patrick Henry fired a barrage of negative questions in one of the most famous speeches in U.S. history. In an effort to persuade his audience to vote to prepare for war in his famous "Give Me Liberty or Give Me Death" speech, he said:

They tell us, sir, that we are weak; unable to cope with so formidable an adversary. But when shall we be stronger? Will it be next week or next year? Will it be when we are totally disarmed, and when a British guard shall be stationed in every house? Shall we gather strength by irresolution and inaction?

Rhetorical questions must be used with some caution. Except in unusual cases, they must be truly rhetorical and neither demand nor permit a verbal response from an audience. Audiences are quite reluctant to give an overt, honest answer to a speaker. Listeners tend to be passive, and if the speaker asks, "Let me see the hands of those who support safe driving," the response may be far from accurate. And it may cause the speaker to look foolish if the next sentence in the speech is based on a response that did not materialize. Just as bad is the question that does get an audible response when none is desired. If a writer expects listeners to be boisterous, unfriendly, or drunk, rhetorical questions may not be wise.

Zingers

A zinger is a sort of rhetorical bumper sticker that makes a point in a clever, popular, and sometimes humorous manner. It usually involves obvious word play, and it usually can be quoted without knowing the context of the speech. A sample somewhat longer than usual was delivered by Norman D. Potter of Cities Service Company at a state Jaycees meeting: "Scientists say that giants no longer walk the earth. They may be right, but Jaycees are leaving some mighty big foot prints" (Potter 1980, 181). In a short zinger, Congresswoman Shirley Chisholm said, "Not failure, but low aim, is sin" (Chisholm 1978, 671).

President Gerald Ford had a standard zinger he could insert as needed in speeches on political subjects: "And don't forget that a government big enough to give you everything you want is big enough to take away everything you have!" Jay Van Andel, speaking as chairman of the U.S. Chamber of Commerce, used a variation on Ford's theme with a zinger: "Remember, when someone gets something for nothing, someone else gets nothing for something" (Van Andel 1979, 556).

Alliteration

A little alliteration can enliven a speech. If it is overdone—and the previous sentence approaches the boundary—it will annoy. The following phrase from an early draft of a speech offers an excellent opportunity for adding alliteration: "Oil companies are making huge investments in modernizing refineries." The word *huge* should probably be replaced because it is a loaded word that should not appear in a sentence sympathetic to oil companies. Replacing it with *major*—a word with more positive connotations—permits a modest level of alliteration with *making* and *modernizing*. The *m* sound in *investments* does not get enough stress to overdo the alliteration.

Alliteration may be used for words in a sequence of ideas or even in wording main points. Paul Wise, president of the Alliance of American

Insurers, for example, developed a five-point speech on arson control using the words *commitment, creativity, creditibility, courage,* and *coordination* (Wise 1978, 61-64).

Balance

The zingers by President Ford and Jay Van Andel illustrate balance in sentence structure. So does the *ask not* line from John F. Kennedy's Inaugural Address. All three apply the classic formula, AB—BA, that may be best known in such advertising slogans as, "You can take Salem out of the country, but you can't take the country out of Salem." Dow writer Carl Shafer made use of this formula in his observation that "educators make simple things complex—but teachers make complex things simple" (Shafer 1985, 15).

As in the case of alliteration, this device must not be overused. If too many balanced sentences are included, a speech will have a singsong sound. Also, balance should not be an end in itself; the form must not overcome substance as it did in the case of the protester carrying a sign reading, "Power, yes. Power plants, no."

The rhetorical devices discussed here are the most important of those available, but more may be used. Hyperbole, parallelism, and onomatopoeia are other devices.

SPECIAL CONSIDERATIONS IN LANGUAGE

Problems in Hearing Words

The English language creates a few traps for the unwary speaker. Words that sound alike but have different meanings are instantly clear in print but not in speech. "The Jimmy Carter era" may, depending on the speaker's pronunciation, sound the same as "The Jimmy Carter error." "An expensive site" is heard by some as "an expensive sight." And the speaker who said of the woman he was introducing, "She and her entire family have this special something in their genes" did not realize that many people in his audience would hear the last word as *jeans*.

The phrase *in sufficient numbers* may seem to some to be *insufficient numbers*. The list could be expanded to include *in adequate, in appropriate,* and *in sensible*. The listener will correct the mistake when the context of the words becomes clear, but there will be a momentary problem.

Words difficult for the speaker to pronounce should be avoided. President Ford had the habit of adding an extra syllable to *judgment*, and President Carter never seemed to master *nuclear*. Almost any speaker will have trouble with tongue twisters where *r* and *w* sounds are put too close together or where a number of *s* sounds give the speech a hissing quality.

Attribution of Quotations

In essays or reports, quotations are often written with the "he said" or "she said" in the middle to break up the monotony of the quotation. Sometimes the attribution appears at the end. Neither of these approaches works well in speaking. The following passage, if read aloud, will show the problem:

"You can never," he said, "make up your mind about anything."
"Oh, I don't know about that," I replied.

In normal speech, the exchange would read something like this:

He said, "You can never make up your mind about anything," and I said, "Oh, I don't know about that."

For the most part, synonyms for *said* should be avoided, but at times such words as *noted*, *pointed out*, *observed*, *contended*, or *wrote* will help establish the tone of the material to be quoted. In humorous material especially, writers will often find awkward substitutions for *said* in print: "he sputtered" or "he responded gamely." *Said* is almost always safer.

If a speaker has the ability to use vocal inflection to mark the quoted material, *said* can be—like *quote* and *unquote*—omitted altogether: "Let's see what Joe Jones had to say on that point" or "Here's Joe Jones's opinion."

Although any quotation a speaker uses will necessarily have been made in the past, a convention in public speaking allows for use of the present tense. It may make a quotation sound slightly more dramatic to say, "As Joe Jones puts it" or "Joe Jones writes in his new book that . . . "

Loaded Language

A professor of rhetoric once observed, "Language is sermonic." Words preach. The language used in discussion of social and political issues will seldom be neutral. Writers must have a sensitivity to loaded language. They should avoid using words loaded against the arguments they make, and they should choose the most positive terms available that will give honest support to their claims.

A writer for a corporation, for example, will find that many terms in common use reflect negatively on business. To take a well-known example, the word *profit* should not appear in an incidental context in a business speech to the general public. Unless a speech discusses profit directly, casual references to the concept will frequently be made with such terms as *earnings* or *return on investment*. Substitution solves the problem.

As an alternative to substitution, negatively loaded terms can be qualified when they are used. The term *consumer advocate*, for instance, is a highly loaded phrase. It suggests someone standing up for the rights of all consumers even though some individuals who acquire the label represent only a small number of consumers. A business speaker who refers to such a person must qualify the term either directly by discussing the label or indirectly by prefacing it with a limiting phrase, such as *so-called*. Oil industry speakers, for example, routinely explain or qualify the term *windfall profits tax*.

Where possible, negative terms should be replaced with positive ones. *Major investments* rather than *huge investments* illustrates this approach. A writer in the electric power field should not refer to higher rates during peak hours as a "penalty." The industry strategy for encouraging conservation would be better expressed by the word *incentive*.

Another aspect of loaded language might be called the you-we-they problem. Almost never will a speaker get a fair hearing by saying, "The trouble is you are not working hard enough." To avoid creating a communication barrier, the speaker would have to move at least as far as the *we* on the scale and perhaps in some caes as far as the *they*. However, it would not be wise to say, "Our customers [they] will benefit" when the speaker could say, "You will benefit." Generally, "you" get the good news, "they" get the bad news, and "we" get the challenges.

When facing almost any tough issue, writers will discover that opposition speakers and writers take full advantage of the sermonic nature of language. Most speaking finds its justification in society's advocacy approach to resolving problems: two sides debate, and the public decides. If an argument is logical and honest, it should be stated in language that makes the case in the most positive manner possible.

CONCLUSION

No feature of speech writing presents a greater challenge to a writer's abilities than does language. The suggestions in this chapter highlight some of the problems writers face. The problems can be solved not by an easy formula but by hours of writing and rewriting.

7

Applying a Touch of Humor

The wit that suits the orator is rare.
 —Quintilian, Roman teacher of rhetoric

Modern speech writers cannot afford to ignore the role of humor in communication. The demand for good humor in speeches has never been greater. Many corporate officers are no longer willing to settle for a few tired jokes in opening a speech. They now insist on having the quality of humor they see not merely in entertainment but increasingly in outstanding business and political speeches.

Bob Orben points out, "Humor has often been the key that unlocks an audience's receptivity" (Orben, 1982, 3). Orben, who in addition to heading President Ford's speech writing staff, has written for comedians Red Skelton, Jack Parr, and Dick Gregory, takes humor seriously. In writing humor for speakers and in conducting workshops for speakers and speech writers, he finds a steady demand for his professional advice on choosing and using humor in speeches.

Speech writers can purchase publications offering current humor—Orben's *Current Comedy* is one excellent source—or they can buy tailor-made humor at prices that may range from a few hundred to a few thousand dollars. Only a few speech writers will actually need to write original humor, but even that is possible by reworking a piece of humor or by creating humor with a standard formula such as the good news–bad news idea.

Whatever approach a writer takes, some thinking about humor will be advisable. And that thinking should start with a consideration of some of the problems that must be confronted in adding humor to speeches.

PROBLEMS

Writers will have great difficulty knowing what an audience will consider funny. Even professional comedians sometimes fail to get a laugh with material supplied by highly competent comedy writers. Most speech writers lack a professional's sense of comedy, and most of the speakers they write for are far from professional in the timing skills required in the delivery of humorous material.

When humor does fail, the results can be devastating to the speaker and to the success of the remainder of the speech. The silence following the punch line will seem like an eternity. The only thing worse than complete silence would be the sound of the speaker laughing alone.

Humor, which often depends on an element of exaggeration and a willing suspension of disbelief, may be completely misunderstood. Some listeners will accept in dead seriousness an idea intended to be funny. This confusion is seen when a delightful piece of satire appears in a newspaper only to be followed a few days later by a letter to the editor from a reader who completely missed the point.

Some studies have found that humor can cause speakers to lose credibility. This is a complicated matter, but it may be that a serious effort at persuasion will be jeopardized by innocent humor. Perhaps it was this problem that caused the nineteenth-century U.S. senator Tom Corwin to warn, "Never make people laugh. If you would succeed in life, you must be solemn as an ass. All the great monuments are built over solemn asses."

VALUE OF HUMOR

In spite of these problems, writers have a wide range of reasons for including a humorous touch in a speech. For one thing, the speaker may demand it. An adamant, "Put me a couple of jokes in there," may settle the issue. Or the situation may call for humor, even if both speaker and writer would prefer to avoid it. If all the events preceding the speech take place in an atmosphere of fun and games, a speaker can hardly make an abrupt shift to somber material.

If humor succeeds in a speech, the payoff will be significant. Humor can help hold an audience's attention and can revive a tired, listless group of listeners. A laugh or a smile produces an interaction with the speaker, and when something strikes them as funny, members of an audience often become more alert by looking at one another and responding to the reactions of others. As Quintilian expressed it in the first century A.D., the effect of humor on the listener is that of "diverting his mind from too intense application to the subject before it, recruiting at times its powers, and reviving it after disgust and fatigue." In other words, humor wakes up the audience.

A light touch can go a long way in revealing a speaker's friendliness and goodwill. After he lost an important political battle, John F. Kennedy showed he was a good sport by telling a rather old joke. Kennedy said following his defeat, he felt much like the western pioneer who was shot full of arrows and left alone on the prairie: "It only hurts when I laugh."

Humor, properly used, can drive home a point. When Carl E. Reichardt, president of Wells Fargo, wanted to criticize excessive reliance on efforts to measure the money supply in making financial decisions, he used humor to attack the complex formulas based on "M-1A, M-B, M-2 [and] M-3." He said, "One group of economists contends that adding all these various types of transactions together to get a money supply figure is like adding roller skates, pogosticks, and subway trains to arrive at a total number for transportation vehicles in the U.S." (Reichardt 1981, 730).

Thus, in spite of its problems, humor does have its place. Writers can benefit from the occasional use of humor if they understand its distinctive role in communication and take a few basic precautions.

SPECIAL NATURE OF HUMOR IN COMMUNICATION

Some comparisons have already been made between speech humor and humor used by comedians. Humor by a stand-up comic on the "Tonight Show" or the humor in a skit in a variety program have something in common with the humor found in speeches. But the fundamental purposes of the professional entertainer and the speaker differ sharply.

One of the biggest mistakes a speaker can make is to judge the success of humor in communication on the basis of the amount of the laughter it gets. That sort of measurement is appropriate for an entertainer. One professional humor writer has suggested a good comedy routine should generate five laughs a minute. The number of laughs, along with their duration and volume, gives us a ready means of knowing if a comedian is "truly funny." In fact, one comic has a clever bit in which he plaintively criticizes the "silent laughers" who, to be polite, place their hands over their mouths to keep their merriment from being audible.

Humor in a speech is judged by a different standard. The amount of overt audience response does not matter as much as the effect of the humor on the total success of the speech. The writer needs to ask whether humor will attract and hold attention, make a point clear, help the audience see that the speaker is a caring, friendly person. To achieve these results, smiles and chuckles may do the job as well as or better than roars of laughter.

Humor in communication, then, cannot be viewed as an end in itself. This is not to say that humor can never be the major vehicle for an argument. Aristophanes attacked the philosophy of Socrates in theatrical comedy, and Jonathan Swift made social and political points with satire.

"Doonesbury," like many other comic strips before it, uses biting humor to take sides on current events. Some newspapers refuse to run this strip on the comics page because it argues while it entertains. They treat it as an editorial cartoon because it seems to be more argument than entertainment.

Conversely, a speaker should not be placed in the role of entertainer when the occasion calls for persuasion. If humor in a speech is excessive, if it is perceived as an end and not a means, the speaker has become a comic. In that role, arguments lose their punch. *Gulliver's Travels* would have been mere entertainment. Senator Corwin's statement that monuments are built over "solemn asses" was an irrepressibly comic reflection of his belief that his heavy-handed use of jokes had adversely affected his political career.

TYPES OF HUMOR

Too often writers and speakers think of humor as consisting only of jokes. The joke, or humorous anecdote, is but one of the types of humor available. It has its place but should not be overused.

Humorous Anecdote

Jimmy Durante used to say, "Everybody wants to get into the act." Ordinary people get into the comedy act with jokes; children bring them home from school; adults tell them at parties and at the office. Anyone can tell a joke, and everyone is a critic. That is both the strength and the weakness of jokes in speeches. Audiences find the joke a comfortable, familiar form of humor, but because they have heard and told so many—including bad ones—a speaker faces a difficult assignment when called on to deliver a joke.

Introducing a humorous story in a speech can create a problem. In setting up a joke, the old "a funny thing" approach should be avoided. Any claim that the joke will be funny puts the audience in a "show me" frame of mind. "That reminds me" makes an equally weak beginning. The joke should be introduced without any special fanfare. It should begin the same as any other supporting material in the speech.

Three fairly typical jokes suitable for speeches appear below. With one exception, they start out well. But because the jokes have not been adequately edited for the ear, they contain problems: the punch lines are sometimes cluttered with extra words at the end, clauses interrupt the flow of some of the sentences, awkward-sounding synonyms for *said* are used in some cases, the placement of attribution of quoted words is in the wrong place, and some of the language is for the eye and not the ear. Each joke will be presented in its print version and then shown as it might be edited for the ear.

[Print version:] I try to keep in mind the story about Frankie Albert, the former 49er football player, who was speaker at a father-and-son dinner. After the speech, he answered all questions thrown at him by the kids. One boy kept raising his hand until he caught Frankie's eye. "And what's your question, sonny?" asked Albert.

"What's next on the program?" the kid said.

[Oral version:] I try to keep in mind the story about the former 49er football player Frankie Albert. He was once giving a speech at a father-and-son dinner, and after the speech he agreed to answer any question the kids wanted to ask. One boy kept raising his hand until finally Frankie saw him and said, "And what's your question, sonny?"

"The kid said, "What's next on the program?"

The biggest problem in the written version is the placement of the attribution on the punch line. "The kid said" comes at the point the audience should begin to laugh; it steps on the laughter. In the oral version, one clause has been eliminated (line 2) and the slightly difficult "asked Albert" has been altered.

[Print version:] One of old coach George Halas's funniest stories has as its hero the Chicago Bear immortal, tackle George Musso. One afternoon Musso was flattened by a terrific block. The trainer dashed onto the field, while a stretcher crew poised for action on the sidelines.

When the trainer reached Musso, he found him just regaining consciousness. "How do you feel?" the trainer asked anxiously.

"Okay," replied the huge tackle. "But how's the crowd taking it?"

[Oral version:] One of old coach George Halas's stories has as its hero the Chicago Bear immortal, tackle George Musso. One afternoon Musso was flattened by a terrific block. The trainer ran out on the field, and a stretcher crew was poised for action on the sidelines.

When the trainer got to Musso, he found him just regaining consciousness, and he said, "How do you feel?"

Musso said, "I'm okay, but how's the crowd taking it?"

This joke, alone of samples shown here, promises in the opening line of the original version that it will be funny. In addition, it puts the attribution either in the middle or at the end of the quoted words rather than at the start. And it has some words and phrases that look good in print but do not sound as conversational as required by a joke. For example, few people in conversation would say "the trainer dashed onto the field." Also, spoken humor does not need the word *anxiously* to explain how the trainer asked his question. The speaker's voice should convey the anxiety; if the emotion is not in the speaker's voice, the term *anxiously* will only make matters worse.

[Print version:] We've been like the hound dog in an Ozark story. The hound was sitting in a country store and howling his head off. A stranger came in and said to the storekeeper, "What's the matter with that howlin' dog?"

"He's sittin' on a cockleburr," said the storekeeper.

"Why doesn't he get off?" the stranger asked.

"He'd rather howl," came the answer.

[Oral version:] We've been like the hound dog in an Ozark story. The hound was sitting in a country store howling his head off. A stranger came in and said to the storekeeper, "What's the matter with that howlin' dog?"

The storekeeper said, "He's sittin' on a cockleburr."
The stranger said, "Why doesn't he get off?"
The storekeeper shook his head and said, "He'd rather howl."

This anecdote has only two problems with its language. The first is, once again, with attribution. That can be solved by moving the attribution to the beginning of the sentences. The second problem comes with setting up the punch line. The four pieces of the dialogue come too quickly and too evenly for the punch line to stand out in the printed version. This is no problem to the reader who sees where the punch line falls on the page. But listeners need to hear the buildup that lets them know the end is coming. If the speaker has the ability to handle it, the last three attributions could be eliminated altogether, leaving only the dialogue to carry the humor.

The three jokes have been rewritten and examined in detail because they are fairly typical of the jokes writers find in print and transfer into speeches with too little editing. Many writers seem to treat a printed joke as though it were a quotation or a statistic—something that the writer has no authority to alter. That attitude should not prevail in using jokes; they must often be rewritten to suit the demands of oral style.

When a speaker delivers the punch line in a joke, a crucial point has been reached. In an interview on humor, Bob Orben pointed out that an inexperienced speaker may not wait long enough for the audience to respond. Orben recommends that rather than rushing on after a pause of a second or two, the speaker should attempt to force a laugh by waiting. He also suggests having a few quips or "savers" ready to turn the failure of a joke into a laugh (Costello 1978, 42). Johnny Carson is master at getting a good laugh with a quick comment on the failure of a joke.

Writers can help speakers cope with potential failure by providing a cover line after a joke. The cover line can be especially valuable for speakers who must follow the manuscript closely because they cannot or will not ad-lib. A cover line comes immediately after the punch line. It consists of a brief comment on the joke, and it can serve either of two functions. If the joke is successful and gets a good reaction, the cover line will be perceived as a response to the audience's appreciation of the humor. If the joke dies, the cover line justifies the joke that did not prove to be funny and serves as a bridge from the wreckage of the joke back to the body of the speech.

A cover line for the Frankie Albert joke might be, "You have to admire honesty even when it hurts." This cover line would be almost a throwaway if it came following gales of laughter or a few dozen broad smiles. In those cases it would be saying, "We all understand kids, don't we?" But the line would be much more valuable if the joke got only blank stares from the listeners. Then the line would say, "Here is why I told you that story" and would permit the speaker to move on. A cover line for the Musso story might be, "Now that's what I'd call loyalty to the fans" and for the Ozark story, "I guess we've all run into that attitude before." The content of the cover line depends on the point being made in the joke and the next idea in the speech. Although not every speaker—or every joke—requires a cover line, the device may come in handy when a writer thinks a speaker may need an avenue of escape.

The One-liner

In many respects, the one-liner is a much better vehicle for humor than the joke because it gets the humorous point made quickly. Although *one-liner* is a misnomer—this form of humor may require two or three sentences—it still does not require the involved buildup needed in jokes. It fits the fast-paced mood of modern times.

When President Carter stated publicly, "I'll whip his ass," in reference to his campaign against Ted Kennedy, the one-line response from Kennedy was, "I knew the President was behind me, but I didn't know how close." Kennedy won the exchange, if not the nomination.

Abraham Lincoln often expressed an idea with a one-liner. When one of the several inept generals he appointed was asked where his headquarters was to be, the general replied, "My headquarters will be in the saddle." Lincoln at once recognized that the general had more style than ability and observed, "He's got his headquarters where his hindquarters ought to be."

Governor Mario Cuomo slipped a one-liner into his Harvard University commencement address when he wanted to make the point that many people misunderstand the university: "They think all Harvard graduates look like Arthur Schlesinger and sound like Ted Kennedy" (Cuomo 1985, 582).

A one-liner can be an excellent substitute for the joke many speakers feel they need at the beginning of a speech. Beginning a talk before the Economic Club of Detroit, Howard M. Love, president of National Steel, said, "I remind myself that the secret to survival for speakers at The Economic Club of Detroit is similar to the secret to survival of the pedestrian in downtown Detroit traffic . . . there are the quick . . . and the dead. I plan to be quick!" (Love 1981, 216).

Integrated Humor

Although both the one-liner and the joke may carry a message, humor is their dominant element. First and foremost, the speaker is saying something funny. Integrated humor reverses the roles of humor and substance. This type of humor states an idea in a clever way, but the idea is stronger than the humor. Unlike the joke or the one-liner, the idea in integrated humor should be strong enough to stand on its own.

Richard G. Capen of Knight-Ridder Newspapers told a college audience that he thought it a tragedy when someone achieves a career goal "and then looks back to wonder whether the trip was worth the price. Some such individuals find that they have climbed ladders propped up against the wrong walls'' (Capen 1980, 766).

Peter G. Peterson, chairman of Lehman Brothers Kuhn Loeb, explained the difficulty Americans have in understanding some foreign countries by saying, "The Third World has always been what in the Nixon Administration we called a MEGO subject ('mine eyes glaze over') in terms of U.S. domestic politics" (Peterson 1980, 137).

When Harry Gray of United Technologies Corporation wanted to make the point that times have changed, he found integrated humor a useful tool:

In the summer of 1936 I unloaded fruit crates for 10 dollars a week. Of course, a dollar was worth something in those days. You could buy a loaf of bread for 9 cents. When you went to buy some meat, the friendly butcher would throw in a portion of liver for the cat—which the cat never got. Nowadays, if you go to an expensive restaurant in Chicago, a portion of liver costs $18. When I was in college there wasn't a man alive who could *lift* $18 worth of liver! (Gray 1984, 526)

Gray did not tell a joke. He did not, in the ordinary sense of the term, use a one-liner. He simply illustrated his point with a humorous idea cleverly worded. His content and his humor were thoroughly integrated. This type of humor offers extremely low risk to the speaker because if it were not funny at all, it would still support the speaker's case. Of course, there is every reason to expect that an audience would find the story quite funny.

Poems, Puns, and Pranks

Poems. It is hard to say what has killed poetry in our society. One good explanation may be that the parent slowly smothered the child as poets over the years have grown increasingly obscure. At any rate, the good has gone down with the bad, and even the delightful comic verse of the Ogden Nash and Richard Armour type is out of vogue. Almost all good limericks are too dirty to use in public, and the humor in the lyrics of popular songs is seldom intentional. The speech writer has little material available and few audiences attuned to humor in verse.

Occasionally, however, a poem can help make a point with a touch of humor. Speaking for the U.S. Education Department, Donald Senese (1985, 426) enlivened a speech with a centuries-old poem by Robert Southey:

> And everybody praised the duke
> Who this fight did win
> But what good came of it at last?
> Quoth little Peterkin
> "Why, that I cannot tell, said he:
> "But 'twas a famous victory"

Puns. Almost never can a writer include a pun in a speech. A speech with a pun would almost certainly have to be intended purely for entertainment in a situation such as a roast. Puns invite groans, and speakers should not be deliberately exposed to a negative audience response. The temptation to use a pun may arise, but it should be suppressed.

Pranks. Except for highly specialized speeches, few opportunities arise for a speaker to use unusual dress, pratfalls, or comic visual aids to get laughter. Perhaps in an in-house safety talk, a stooge might be brought in covered with fake bandages and a leg cast. Or to lighten a fund-raising talk, a chart might depict a dollar bill being stretched or squeezed. But the opportunities for such unconventional devices are rare. They usually exist with "in" groups and depend on having a speaker who can avoid turning into a buffoon.

Using a professional magician or a clown to make a presentation or designing comic visual aids may be effective, but it involves a type of communication beyond the scope of the present subject.

The distinctions among the types of humor discussed here may sometimes be hard to recognize. A long one-liner may be very much like a joke. If a writer quotes Gray's story about changing times, a piece of integrated humor will have become an anecdote. The point here, however, has not been to construct perfect classifications. The mechanics of classifying are less important than recognition of a great variety of available humor. Writers will find it especially valuable to remember that humor extends beyond the joke.

TESTS FOR HUMOR

Before any type of humor finds it way into a speech, it should pass three tests: relevancy, taste, and freshness.

Relevancy

Too many speakers begin with a few jokes and then say, in effect, "Now that the humor is over, I'll give my speech." Even if the jokes are funny, the audience's attention has been gained with a false start, and some listeners may feel they have been misled.

Equally bad is the speaker who abruptly says, "That reminds me of . . ." and then wedges unrelated humor into a talk. Humor should be an integral part of a speech. It should clarify an idea or emphasize a point. Al Capp, for example, was making an argument when he said that a college president who thinks the students are better able to run the school than the president is probably right.

Taste

A study of the history of humor bears out what anyone knows who hears jokes on the job: vulgarity and cruelty appear with regularity in humor. These two features supply much of the shock value needed to make some humor work.

The difference between the private telling of offensive humor and its exposure in public can be seen in the widely publicized jokes told a few years back by former cabinet officer Earl Butz. His jokes were no worse than those told every day in offices and at parties, but once they were revealed to the public, there was a roar of protest. On a much smaller scale, a speech writer should remember that a joke that depends for its humor on having a fat man in it will not necessarily sound offensive in the office. But when the speaker begins to read the joke to an audience and notices three stout people in the front row, both the speaker and the audience will be embarrassed.

The number of groups with increased consciousness of their identity accompanied by an increased sensitivity to being the target of humor appears to be growing. Gray awareness and gay awareness are but two current examples. To be safe, only blacks can tell jokes about blacks, and the right to poke fun at school teachers should be reserved to those who teach school.

Only recently have efforts been made to measure possible negative effects on speakers who use self-disparaging humor. One such study examined the impact on an audience when speakers explained the value of their professions but in the process used humor that had those professions as its target. One of the speeches defended the field of economics while including deprecating humor such as the one-liner, "If all economists were laid end to end, they would still each point in a different direction" (Chang and Gruner 1981, 421). The study found no significant negative reaction to the self-disparaging humor. The authors did, however, suggest two precautions with humor of this sort. They warn that the humor may not be successful unless the speaker is perceived by the audience as a highly respected person, and they caution that in the process of the speaker's disparaging the speaker's own group, no strongly held beliefs of the audience should be held up to ridicule.

Humor at the speaker's expense seems safe. Richard Nixon used a self-deprecating remark as he started to rebuild his political fortunes following his 1960 series of television confrontations with John F. Kennedy. Recognizing that Kennedy's performance helped decide the election, Nixon quipped, "I'm a dropout from the electoral college. I flunked debate."

Freshness

Those who say there's no such thing as a new joke may be right. Humor has a way of spreading quickly over a wide region and then of cropping up after going through a dormant period. And, after all, most humor fits into a few basic formulas.

Since speech writers do not often create humor but rather adapt existing material, they need to be especially concerned about using stale wit. A stale joke is not the same as an old joke. A good story from the current *Reader's Digest* is likely to be stale because many people have heard or read it. A piece of humor from a two-year-old copy of the *Digest* will be old but possibly quite usable.

The following sample of humor could easily be updated to apply to the conflict between the Poles and the Soviets that figured heavily in the news about controversy over Polish labor unions in the 1980s. The story was widely told in the early 1950s. The dialogue is between a Communist official and a pupil from a Polish school:

"Who is your father?"
"Stalin, the father of all progress."
"Very good, and who is your mother?"
"The Soviet Union, mother of all peace-loving people."
"Splendid! Now, tell me, my little fellow. What would you like to be when you grow up?"
"An orphan."

One way to meet the need for fresh humor is to draw material from the speaker's personal or business experience. Almost everyone has a collection of "funny things that happened to me" stories. These incidents are usually not funny enough to be sold to the *Digest*, but their weaknesses are compensated for by the fact that they really happened.

An especially good sample of a personal anecdote can be found in the speech, "Humor Is Serious Business" by comedy writer and humorist Gene Perrett. He told the story of going with Bob Hope to the airport to meet Mrs. Hope's flight:

She was flying in from Palm Springs on a private plane. Dolores Hope is very active in Catholic charities in Palm Springs, Los Angeles, and many other places, and many of her friends are Catholic priests. When we got to the airport the plane came up, the little steps came down, and the first two people off the plane were Catholic priests. Then came Dolores Hope, and then came four more Catholic priests. Bob Hope nudged me and said, "I don't know why she just doesn't buy insurance like everybody else." (Perrett 1985, 651).

The president of New York Telephone, D. C. Staley, found a story from his experience valuable in the opening of a speech:

They tell the story of a Bell System executive who showed up for a speaking occasion. As he approached the banquet hall, someone called out—"The telephone man is here." The hotel manager, standing nearby, turned to an assistant and said, "That was fast. Show him where to install it."

That may sound like telephone fiction—but I want you to know that I missed out on the prime ribs that day. (Staley 1980, 29)

The effort to personalize humor should not extend to lying. Often a speaker will say something like, "There was this Baptist preacher in my home town . . ." and then go on to tell a standard borrowed joke. This practice runs the risk of undermining the speaker's credibility. It should not be used unless the speaker is confident the audience will know from the beginning the story is not to be taken at face value.

SOURCES OF HUMOR

Speech writers who use humor should keep a file of good material. Such a file will help cut down on the frustration of facing a deadline for a speech while plowing through page after page in a published collection of humor. It is unreasonable to expect a quick search to produce suitable humor from such a source. Any humor collection must be broad enough to appeal to thousands of readers; it cannot contain a high percentage of jokes that suit the needs of any one individual.

The few useful bits from a collection should be culled out and filed separately with a good index. Into this system should go the clever items gathered from nonhumor sources such as news stories, magazine articles, and books. (Watch for headlines such as the one proclaiming "Senators for Sale" over a story announcing that two senators were in support of weapons sales to a foreign government.) A writer who over a period of time selects possibly relevant material will find the search process shortened in those crucial hours before a speech draft is due.

Humor can be borrowed from other speeches. It can be jotted down after an amusing incident has occurred in the office. It can be taken from graffiti, bumper stickers, t-shirts, cartoons, comic strips, and comedians on television or radio. And it can be bought from professional writers and compilers of humor.

Orben's *Current Comedy* is a collection of one-liners that over a period of time will yield a large reservoir of appropriate humor. Recorded speeches on humor and humorous topics by Art Fettig and Mick Delaney provide writers with material as well as with ideas on the effective use of humor.

Like any other aspect of speech writing, humor requires work and study. The ability to use humor, as Fettig points out, is not something a writer is born with. The suggestions presented in this chapter set forth the basics. Observation and experience take over after that.

8

Coaching the Speaker

Speak the speech, I pray you, as I pronounced it to you, trippingly on
the tongue. But if you mouth it, as many of our players do, I had as lief
the town crier spoke my lines. Nor do not saw the air too much with
your hand, thus, but use all gently. . . . Be not too tame neither; but let
your own discretion be your tutor. Suit the action to the word, the word
to the action.

—*Hamlet* (act II, scene 2)

In discussing the delivery of a speech, where word and action merge, writer
Mike Stott compares a speech writer to a caddy for a pro golfer. The caddy
suffers through every bad shot and rejoices in every good one. And a caddy,
like a writer, has to be prepared to offer sound advice. The writer has one
important limitation that the caddy does not: the writer can make suggestions only during the practice rounds or in the clubhouse afterward. In
actual delivery, speakers are on their own.

PREPARING THE MANUSCRIPT

Typing a manuscript in proper form can help a speaker in delivery by
making it easier for the speaker to use eye contact more freely. The type
should be large, and boldface type will make the page easier to read. Some
speakers have difficulty with all capital letters, so some of the standard
typefaces may not work well for them. An all-cap style also runs the risk of
creating confusion between common and proper nouns.

Only about the upper half or two-thirds of the page should be used to avoid giving the audience a view of the top of the speaker's head as the speaker follows the text to the bottom. Wide left margins of about one-third of the page will be especially helpful for speakers who treat the manuscript as an outline and use it for talking points.

Lines should never be broken at the end of a page. Although it rarely happens, a speaker may skip the page of a talk by mistake, as President Carter once did in a major speech. Unless each page ends with a complete sentence, this bad situation becomes even worse.

If sentences are broken at the end of a page, there will be an artificial pause when the page must be turned. Starting each page with a new sentence has the advantage of making the last line on the previous page easy to pick up and deliver with good eye contact. After all, one of the speaker's major problems will be returning to the correct line after eye contact. If that line is the first one on the next page, the transition can be made smoothly.

In the manuscript, the writer should feel free to ignore traditional rules for paragraphs because only the speaker will see the script. The writer can indent wherever more space would help the speaker see a shift in meaning or phrasing. Some one-sentence paragraphs can be used, or even parts of a sentence can be paragraphed, perhaps with bullets to make the ideas stand out. A speaker's eye can readily pick up such paragraphs from the double-spaced page of a manuscript. Some speakers prefer "outdenting," in which the first line of a paragraph extends into the margin where the eye can readily pick it up.

Words in a speech manuscript should be freely underlined, an especially helpful device in suggesting vocal stress. Speakers who can be encouraged to do their own markings may read with even more feeling than if the underlining were supplied by the writer.

Underlining may help a speaker quickly pick up short passages to deliver without looking at the manuscript. Taking this idea one step further, a zinger might be colored with a highlight pen to help the speaker scoop it up in one glance and to indicate clearly where the reading of the text will resume. Or a line might be arranged on the page with attention to units of thought rather than to grammatical structure, as can be seen by rearranging the previous sentence in this paragraph:

A zinger might be colored with a highlight pen
both to help the speaker scoop it up in one glance
and to indicate clearly
where the reading of the text will resume.

The place to break a sentence on the right margin should always be governed by sense rather than space. It would not be wise, for example, to break a sentence in the following way:

New data came to us last year from Florida
State University.

Speech writers should not feel bound by standard rules for punctuation. Semicolons and colons send rather weak signals to a person reading a speech aloud. They are sometimes hard to see, and a speaker may read a comma as a period, especially when the script has been typed in all caps. Dashes offer a better choice, especially when a forceful clause has been injected into a sentence as in, "Let me respond—and I want no confusion on this point—by saying that our first priority will always be quality."

Depending on what works best for the speaker, pauses may be indicated with three periods or with the word *pause* in parentheses. The use of "(Pause)" can be useful to indicate a break betwen major ideas or to allow time for a touch of humor to get across.

Numbers have to be handled with great care. Terry Smith reports the case of the speaker who read World War II as "World War Eleven" (Smith 1984, 44), and he suggests that all numbers be written out in words. This rule should apply not only to numbers used as support for ideas but also for points, which should not be flagged with 1, 2, 3, or I, II, III, and most especially not with A, B, C. Writing "number one" or "point B in my list" will work much better.

Speakers can be helped with pronunciation by using an approach based on the system in the *NBC Handbook of Pronunciation*. It employs upper case to indicate which syllable gets the stress, and it relies almost exclusively on characters found on the standard keyboard. Some sample words include: Luftwaffe (LŌŎFT vah fuh), Rio de Janeiro (REE ō dā zhuh NĀ rō), Il Duce (eel DŌŌ chā), consul (KAHN s'l), and Pegasus (PĔG uh suhs).

A speech writer may wish to order a specially designed speech portfolio to hold the manuscript. The most widely used of these devices, the Script-Master, is an attractive hinged box about twelve inches high, a bit over nine inches wide, and three-quarters of an inch deep. A speech manuscript placed in the box with pages unbound provides the speaker with a convenient means of carrying the speech. At the lectern, the speaker can open the box like a book. The device eliminates the distraction of turning pages because the speaker can unobtrusively slide each page of the manuscript from the right side to the left into the hinged top of the open box. This technique permits the speaker always to have two pages of the manuscript in view at the same time. (Information for ordering can be found in the appendix.)

A writer may want to arrange for the purchase of a lectern with a built-in microphone to give the speaker a consistent and dependable amplification system. Several brands are available, and all are portable models that can readily be transported and set up wherever the speaker may travel. Although especially useful for in-house speeches, the general unreliability of microphones in most hotel meeting rooms may justify making a portable lectern part of the baggage carried by a speaker's advance agent in public talks as well.

REHEARSING THE SPEECH

Not even a skilled, experienced speaker can expect to deliver a speech well without practice. If a speech writer can develop a good coaching relationship with the speaker, the writer can help ensure that rehearsals are productive. For any important speech, it would be helpful to have two rehearsals of the speech after the final draft has been approved.

Several days before the speech is to be presented, a dry run should be held with the writer present. The dry run could be especially valuable if complicated visuals are to accompany the speech. Even if the visuals are not fully ready, the dry run begins to acquaint the speaker with the talk and with how it will be presented. The writer has the chance to fine-tune the language of the speech.

As close as possible to the date of delivery, the speech should be presented again, this time in a dress rehearsal. All elements of the actual speech should be duplicated as far as is practical. The speech should be read as many times as it takes for the speaker to be comfortable with it and for the writer to make final adjustments.

Opinions differ on the sources to which a speaker should turn for counsel on the techniques of delivery. Advice from family members or colleagues without professional backgrounds in communication can present problems. Such people often are reluctant to point out weak features of a speech and in addition may give irrelevant or even wrong advice. A speaker who comes back to the office with a collection of bad suggestions from a spouse or a friend puts the speech writer in an awkward position.

But most speakers do need coaching, and the writer should seek to conduct it or at the least to control it. The only people present at a practice session should be those who know enough about speech presentation to make intelligent suggestions and who will be candid in their remarks.

Recording the Practice Session on Videotape

A critique of a speaker's dry run and dress rehearsal will be especially valuable if recorded on videotape, but care must be taken to use the practice session to its fullest advantage.

A studio setting should be avoided. Technicians tampering with lights and mikes will distract the speaker. The simplest kind of camera available should be used with normal room lighting, and the microphone should be adjusted before the practice begins (with no interruption at the start of the speech caused by the need to attach a mike to the speaker's clothing). The setting should be a conference room or large office. The key word for the operator of the equipment is *unobtrusive*.

After the practice run has been recorded and before viewing the tape, the speech writer should engage the speaker in a discussion of the effectiveness of the presentation. It will be useful to have two pads or two chalkboard sections on which key performance points can be listed.

The critique should begin by listing the positive features of the presentation. The speaker may wish to dwell on the negative, but an effort should be made to itemize first the aspects of the practice that went well. The writer should add to the list as the discussion progresses. If others have been invited to take part in the critique, they can be asked for comment after the speaker has had the opportunity to contribute.

The videotape does not catch everything of importance. For example, it is quite difficult to tell much about eye contact from the tape. The picture will show only if the speaker is looking down; it will not show if eye contact was made with a listener. Position of the feet, which may affect posture, will usually be left out of the picture.

The second list should be made up of features that can be improved. In a critique, the greatest care must be taken to report honestly on the areas of needed improvement and to avoid wounding the speaker's feelings. Speaking is a personal matter; the ego is involved. Therefore descriptions of weaknesses in delivery should not be discussed with such terms as *bad*, *weak*, or *unsatisfactory*. If eye contact does not appear adequate, "more" should be called for. If the gestures are too small, the writer's recommendation should again be in positive language with the suggestion that "they should be up higher and more obvious to the audience." Distracting mannerisms can be discussed with such terms as "can be avoided" or "does not add to the effectiveness of the speech."

This is not to suggest that a good critique overlooks areas of weakness. These areas should be made obvious. Most speakers, who after all can see the problems for themselves when viewing the tape, appreciate specific suggestions. A surprising number of such speakers are surrounded by advisers who lack the courage to say anything that can be interpreted as bad news.

Uncomfortable silences may occur during the listing stage of the critique, but the listing should not be done hastily. A speaker may be holding back a comment—especially if it is a positive one, that will come out only if extra time is allowed.

After the lists have been compiled, the tape should be run. The tape can be stopped at various points when one of the good features or one of the features that needs improvement appears (it does not have to be stopped at all of them because some comments can be made while the tape is running). When the tape is stopped, the speaker should be encouraged to verbalize the criticism. The basic aim of the critique is to get the speaker involved in the evaluation, with the long-range goal of having the speaker in the habit of monitoring the progress of a speech during delivery.

Viewing a tape of a speech can be a complex event for a speaker. The critique should not be rushed. It will be a good idea to turn the sound off at a point or two so the speaker may concentrate solely on physical behavior. Without the audio, the speaker's gestures, posture, and facial expression will stand out sharply.

When a speaker needs a great deal of improvement or when criticizing a speech of considerable importance, it may be wise to record more than one dress rehearsal performance. The additional practice may be recorded immediately while the needed changes are fresh in the speaker's mind, or it may be best to delay the next practice session to give the speaker time to reflect on the best way to deliver the speech. Circumstances will dictate the best approach.

Helping the Speaker with Audiovisuals

Part of the coaching function will be to give advice on the use of visual aids. This function actually begins with the first speaker-writer conference when the speech is being planned. That function will be discussed now, and the handling of visual aids by the speaker will be treated in the next chapter.

One fundamental principle should guide the speech writer: no audiovisual aid should be used merely for what the U.S. Army field manual on military instruction calls "eye wash." If an aid does not help present the idea more clearly than it can be presented without the aid or if it does not add a dimension of credibility or interest, then the aid becomes a distraction that will inhibit the interaction between speaker and audience.

Occasionally a speaker will want to use visual aids on the grounds that everybody does it. Or the speaker may want the aid to serve as a distraction to keep audience attention away from the speaker's real or imagined weaknesses in speaking. Often speakers use visual aids out of habit.

After eliminating all the visual aids that are not needed, the speech writer should consider pressing for fresh and interesting aids. Charts and slides need not be the only aids used. Speakers might be asked to confess their own reaction to the routine use of slides and charts in speeches they have to hear. Except for professional multimedia productions, most slide presentations are dull.

Among the alternatives to charts and slides, consideration might be given to models and objects. An engineer speaking on the future of energy can increase interest by displaying a piece of oil shale or a jar of tar sand. An executive speaking on government regulation can bring out a stack of documents to demonstrate the paperwork required on a certain project. A speaker on the environment can show samples of water or particles removed from the air. One corporate speaker quoted a favorable comment on his company from *Business Week* by taking the magazine to the lectern to read directly from the source (although the words were also in the manuscript).

Contrary to what many textbooks say, visual aids do not always have to be large enough to be seen in detail. Some aids are used for interest and credibility.

In some cases a speaker should be encouraged to use a large pad, a chalkboard, or an overhead projector to sketch a diagram or to write key words or numbers. Material written during the presentation can enliven the speech if done properly. Only material that can be written quickly should be used; the speaker should keep talking by adding patter to fill the time or by memorizing or paraphrasing a section of the manuscript. A speaker who wanted to show the profit that had been made on an investment gained extra attention in a speech by working the math quickly on a chart rather than showing it on a prepared slide.

Guidelines in Preparing Visual Aids

Keep Visuals Simple. A visual aid displayed to clarify rather than to add credibility or interest must not be cluttered. Each aid should illustrate one idea with a clear point of focus. A somewhat complex aid can be shown by gradually building it up with overlays as the speaker guides the audience through the parts of the picture step by step. The number of "build" slides should be kept to two or three during a talk, or the audience will soon grow tired of this device.

Have a Uniform Format. Kodak suggests that slides supporting a speech should not be a mix of "horizontals, verticals, squares, and circulars" (Kodak 1979, 26). All the artwork on slides and charts should have a consistent style, as should the typeface used in the visuals. When charts and slides are to be exchanged among an organization's speakers and used in more than one speech, a policy on uniform format of visuals can save a lot of duplication of effort and expense.

Make the Aid Visible. Except for aids that do not need to be seen in detail (in the case, for example, of a speaker who brandishes a silicon chip), pictures and charts must be big enough and must be drawn with heavy lines in bold colors. The company audiovisual department will supply aids with these qualities and keep the speaker from having to ad-lib an embarrassed, "I know you can't see this clearly, but. . . ."

The speech writer should see that someone takes the responsibility for making sure that charts and slides will be located in a place where the line of sight is clear. Sometimes slides are not visible because no one has arranged for a way to darken the room or to get electricity to the projector.

Do not Provide Handouts during the Speech. Almost never will it be advisable to pass out material to an audience during a speech. Workshops and training sessions are exceptions, but the normal speech will suffer as members of an audience make their own use of the material. They tend to look at the wrong place when the speaker attempts to focus their attention, and they find handouts suitable for doodling, making grocery lists, and constructing paper airplanes. Especially distracting is the case where a single visual aid is handed out to be passed from listener to listener. If a handout must be distributed, it usually should be made available at the end of the speech.

Avoid Mindless Words, Phrases, and Symbols. Few people appreciate staring at the word PRODUCTIVITY while a speaker discourses on the subject. Nor do filler photographs of the company logo or factory workers at their stations usually give listeners much of value.

Don't Write about the Visual Aids. The language of the speech should deal with ideas, not with the visuals that reinforce but do not replace the substance of the speech. Almost never should the text of a speech have the phrase, "The next slide shows. . . ."

Working with the Audiovisual Experts

Whether employing the services of an audiovisual department within an organization or buying AV material from outside, speech writers need to have a good working relationship with the technicians who supply these services. As in working with someone who furnishes information for speeches, the speech writer will find it useful to get to know the AV experts before they are needed. The capacity of the department or the firm should be understood. Knowing the AV capability will prevent unreasonable expectations and underuse of available talent.

AV technicians work, as speech writers do, under the pressure of deadlines. A writer needs to recognize that pressing demands from others who also need audiovisuals may affect the ability of an in-house department to respond. So just as the writer should expect early notification of a writing assignment from a speaker, the technician should be told of AV needs as soon as possible.

A writer dealing with anyone who is an expert in a technical field must be able to strike a delicate balance. On the one hand, the writer should be open to suggestions and should take advantage of the expertise available. Excellent advice may be offered to improve the quality of the final product. On the other hand, a writer should not be too ready to accept the claim, "It can't be done." A request may be impossible to satisfy, but many times a way can be found if the writer presses the point and has built a good relationship with the AV department.

Preparing for the Question-and-Answer Session

Based on his experience as a White House speech writer, William Safire reported on the preparation required for a president to face a question-and-answer session in the form of a press conference:

The fact is that a presidential press conference requires at least two days of hard homework. [The president's] staff will prepare about 75 questions, covering the approximately 25 that will be asked in a half hour and all those that go unasked. These, along with suggested answers, go into his "black book" for review, occasional challenge and memorization. All presidents of the last two decades have done that homework. (*Richmond Times-Dispatch* 1981, 14)

Safire suggests the general direction to be followed by anyone who wishes to be well prepared before facing a barrage of questions. Supplying a list of questions and answers is the first step.

In addition, the writer playing the role of speech coach may furnish tips on how the Q&A should be handled. Except in the most informal situations, the speaker will find it best to bring the speech to a formal conclusion and turn the program back over to the presiding officer to start the Q&A. This approach allows the speech itself to end on the climactic note the speech writer has included in the final paragraph of the manuscript. The speaker gets a round of applause, and the speaking segment of the program will be over.

If the speaker goes directly into the Q&A session without bringing the speech to a distinct conclusion, the transition is likely to be awkward. The rhythm of almost any Q&A session is slow at the beginning, with a gradual increase in the tempo of responses from the audience as the session progresses. The speaker who remains at the lectern will be in a highly vulnerable spot if there is silence in reply to the offer to answer questions. Speakers at times will throw out fillers that prove to be embarrassing, as illustrated by the weakly stated, "Well, I guess I must have covered things pretty well." It is far better for the speaker to have returned to a seat to allow the person in charge of the program to weather this potentially slow phase of the presentation. After someone is recognized to ask a question, the speaker can return to the stand and take over.

Remembering that the tempo of the Q&A tends to speed up, a speaker should be cautioned to take care in bringing the Q&A to an end. It may be that several hands will be in the air at once when time runs out. To avoid hurting feelings—and also to avoid looking as though the speaker is ducking questions—the speaker should announce a couple of minutes before time expires, "I see we have time for only a few more questions." Then the speaker can safely cut the session off with hands still in the air. Even so, it may be wise, if the speaker can spare the time, to agree to continue to respond to questions after the meeting has adjourned.

The speech writer can help the speaker exit gracefully by writing a brief paragraph to mark the close of the Q&A. This material may consist of a more profuse expression of the speaker's thanks to the audience for being invited than would have been appropriate for the ending of the speech proper. Or the paragraph marking the end of the Q&A can return to the theme or basic points of the speech. However it is handled, it can prevent the speaker from making an awkward exit.

The Q&A session will go more smoothly if everyone in the audience realizes questions are to be allowed after the speech. The printed program and the presiding officer should refer to this fact unless the audience has been fully conditioned to expect a question period following every talk.

Tips on Answering Questions

The writer's role may extend to coaching the speaker on strategy in the techniques of answering questions. Although many trainers offer instruction in this skill, writers are often in the best position to counsel the speaker on which approaches work best in a particular situation. Here are some of the general tips that are often suggested.

Give Short Answers. A speaker may feel an urge to answer the easy questions at great length in order to be protected from the hard ones. Although there is no way to dictate in advance the length of an answer, the rule to follow is keep the answer as short as possible. If all answers are allowed to run as long as three minutes, the standard fifteen-minute question period would permit only five questions to be answered (compare this to the approximately one answer per minute Safire expects the president to answer). An occasional very short answer should be encouraged: "Yes, I fully agree," "No, we would not take that course if we had any other choice," or "Twelve percent last year." If a question is far too complicated to be answered, a speaker is entitled to suggest the direction of the answer in a sentence or two and offer to discuss the matter in private with the questioner. Short answers will be easier to give if the speaker can be trained to start with the heart of the answer rather than attempting to lead up to it.

Say "I Don't Know." If the speaker does not know the answer, a forthright "I don't know" is in order. It is usually wise to offer to find the answer and supply it to the person who asked the question. Few speakers have trouble realizing they do not know the answer to requests for specific data. The biggest danger comes when a broad question dealing with policy or opinion is asked and the speaker thinks the answer may occur while responding. All speakers need to be reminded that off-the-wall questions having nothing to do with the speech may be asked. At least some of these should get the "I don't know" response.

Speakers will face some situations where they should be accompanied by subject matter experts form the organization to deal with narrow technical matters raised in the Q&A. The speaker can respond by saying, "I think that question can best be answered by our vice-president for research and development who is with us this evening."

Repeat the Question. Far too many speakers fail to repeat questions asked too quietly for the audience to hear. Repeating is a courtesy the speaker should extend in large audiences. The speaker may benefit from the slight time allowed to think about the question. Also, questions can often be rephrased in language that is briefer and even somewhat more objective than that in which they were asked. The speaker should not, however, alter the basic meaning of a question.

Don't Plant Questions. Speakers should never arrange to plant questions to take pressure off themselves. Soft questions are easily recognized by the audience and will hurt the speaker's credibility. And if a question is planted in a public meeting, the next day's headlines may include, "Company Plants Stooge in Public Meeting." It may be useful to plant a question, however, if the object is to show that the speaker really intends to be open to whatever the audience wants to ask. A chief executive officer who suspects an employee group will hold back on questions they really care about might have a couple of tough questions planted to get a session started.

Don't Use a Screening Panel. Almost always speakers should allow members of the audience to ask questions in person rather than to submit them through a panel. Even if this were to require, in an in-house speech, arranging for ushers and extra microphones in the audience, the direct personal involvement is a valuable benefit. Few people trust a panel to screen questions fairly, and most would like to speak their concerns for themselves. If, however, there is a concern that listeners may be excessively timid or fearful of retribution, then some provision for anonymous questions may have to be made.

Recognize the Questioner. Once the question period gets underway, the speaker should be in control. A person wishing to ask a question should be recognized directly and positively by the speaker. A speaker can point, call on people by location and/or sex and/or clothing, and can recognize questioners by name or position when known. Questioners should know when they have been called on.

Speakers should take care not to let a few people dominate a session. Some who want to ask questions will indicate their interest with a timid motion of the hand. Speakers need to watch for such people. Special attention needs to be paid to members of the audience sitting at the sides of the room or in the back. It will be best if no one asks a second question until everyone who wants to has had a chance to ask one question.

Facing Hostile Questions

However uncomfortable hostile questions may make a speaker feel, they do have two important benefits. First, they gain the speaker some sympathy. A speaker will seldom face an audience made up entirely of hostile listeners, but even in such a situation, most people will appreciate the speaker's courage. When a hostile minority appears at a meeting, the neutral members of the audience will often express support for a speaker under attack.

Second, the venting process can alter the negative feelings of the hostile questioner. This does not apply to an implacable foe of the speaker, but a typical person who expresses anger in a question to a speaker will go away feeling better about the speaker and the speaker's organization.

When someone asks a nasty question, the speaker should direct the answer not to the person who asked it but to the audience. If the speaker maintains eye contact with the questioner, that person might feel free to interrupt and start an unpleasant dialogue. When ending the answer to any question—especially a hostile one—the speaker should not return to the questioner and ask, "Did that answer your question?"

At times the best way to defuse anger will be to agree with the person who asks the hostile question. When an "Is-it-not-true-that" question brings up a valid point, the speaker should be counseled to agree with the questioner and move on to the next person. Many speakers have an initial impulse to defend publicly everything their organizations do, but an organization's credibility depends more on its candor than on its perfection.

The speaker can show determination in responding to hostility but should not become angry. This is easier said than done, but practice in fielding hostile questions prepared by the speech writer can help. The dangers of not being prepared for hostility can be seen in a case in which a government official was being berated by questioners in a farm audience and in desperation blurted out, "You are lucky to be living in a country where you are free to ask questions like that!" Only rarely will such a display of temper work to a speaker's advantage. Speakers should follow Rudyard Kipling's advice to "keep your head when all about you are losing theirs and blaming it on you."

Even when someone who asks a question is wrong, that person will often feel strongly about the topic being raised. Such a person will be in a much better mood to hear and accept an answer if the speaker can be persuaded to begin by responding to the questioner's feelings before moving on to the answer. A speaker might say, "Well, I can certainly see why you feel the way you do in the light of the information you have" or "If I were in your position, I know I would object just as strongly as you do to that situation."

In many cases, angry people will listen to the speaker's answer only after their feelings have been authenticated—that is, after the speaker concedes that they have the right to be afraid or upset. Then the speaker can move on to give them information to allay concerns that have been accepted as legitimate.

If a hostile question contains loaded words, they have to be avoided in the answer or exposed to the audience as unfair. The answer to the question, "Isn't it true that thermal pollution from your Rocky Creek plant has altered the ecology of Stone Lake?" may be yes. But the negative loading of "thermal pollution" and the negative loading of "altered the ecology" make the correct answer sound negative. The speaker might find it advisable to violate the rule calling for immediately answering the question in a brief sentence or two and instead comment on the language of the question. It might be suggested that the speaker wants the audience to understand that the terms used in the question refer to concepts that might be described in more objective language.

THE SPEECH WRITER AS ADVANCE AGENT

To protect the quality of the speech, the speech writer may find it necessary to precede the speaker to a meeting place to check it out and then to be present to see that all goes well at the meeting. The role of an advance agent varies from speaker to speaker, and each agent needs to have an appropriate checklist to make sure the arrangements are in order.

The duties of an advance agent may run from carrying an extra copy of the manuscript to supplying the speaker with a slice of lemon before the speech. The advance agent will usually be seen in the meeting hall checking the microphone before the audience assembles. Minor changes in the text of the speech may be required if the speaking situation proves to be slightly different from that the writer was led to expect.

Physical Setting

Someone needs to check the room before a speech to make sure it does not create problems for the speaker. A curtain behind the speaker may open onto the hotel swimming pool where the appearance of just one muscle-bound beach boy or a single bikini-clad beauty contestant can blot out half a speech. Distracting flower arrangements, awards trophies, or artwork should be out of sight. The background music should be killed before the speech starts.

There should be adequate lighting on the podium, and no spotlights that blind the speaker with their glare should be permitted. The light level on the speaker should be about the same as that on the audience.

The advance agent should always know the name of a responsible hotel or restaurant management person to contact before the speech to eliminate such problems as removal of dishes at inopportune moments. Members of the speaker's party seldom have any authority over those responsible for unexpected construction noises or other on-site interference. The name of a hotel manager will be most useful in getting such problems solved.

For an important speech, the advance agent should check on events planned for adjoining rooms. Attention should be paid to traffic in hallways. If it cannot be diverted, signs should be posted saying "Meeting in Progress," and doors into the meeting room near the speaker should be closed with "Use Other Entrance" signs on them.

Public Address System and Lectern

The microphone, especially if the speaker does not travel with a portable lectern with built-in amplification, should be checked in advance for quality. The location of the lectern should be checked. The head table may not be the best place from which the speech should be given; instead, the lectern might be set up along the side of the room for best effect. It may be desirable to inform the person in charge of the facility in advance of the way the room should be arranged. Especially for a speech using props or other visual aids, the room should be made to fit the speech instead of the other way around.

Head Table

The speaker should know in advance who will be at the head table and what role each person is to play in the meeting. The name of the presiding officer and the person who will give the speech of introduction should be known to the speaker. The advance agent may find it useful to provide the speaker with brief biographical information about other guests.

The speech of introduction presents special problems. A bad introduction can set the wrong mood and make at least the opening moments of a speech awkward. A speaker will benefit form being provided with an advance copy of the introducer's speech, and, as will be noted in chapter 10, that speech should be written, when possible, by the guest speaker's speech writer.

Press and Publicity

Extensive media coverage of a speech may redefine the audience for the writer. The ultimate target of the talk might be television viewers and newspaper readers. Although this does not mean that the immediate audience can be ignored, presence of the press might substantially affect the aim and content of the body of the speech.

Some writers believe that preparing a press release is the best way to start the speech writing process. For them, a press release puts the central theme of the speech in focus. Other writers take the position that the most news-worthy feature of the speech may not be the most important part of the message.

Another controversy among writers in regard to preparing for press coverage involves the question of when to release the text of a speech. Some regard the predelivery release as a good idea; others fear that this practice cuts down on news coverage. The number of variables to be taken into account in making this decision suggests that no firm rule can be applied. The wisdom of releasing an advance text depends on the circumstances surrounding the speech under consideration.

Both the writer and the speaker should know the extent of press coverage expected. This knowledge will be of psychological value and useful in planning the tone and substance of the talk.

PREPARING FOR THE OVERSEAS SPEECH

Richard Charlton, drawing on his experience in helping speakers prepare for foreign speeches, has sound advice to offer on translation difficulties. He offered his views on that subject as a conclusion for this discussion of the writer's role as advance agent (letter to author).

If a CEO ever needs an advance agent it's in an overseas speech environment. The speech writer or PR director should handle arrangements in advance of the speech to make sure it will achieve the desired goals.

Use instant translation as little as possible. A speech always loses something in translation, and the more instantaneous, the more it loses.

There are often better ways to communicate. For example, on one occasion the president of an American company which had just formed a partnership with a French firm, was invited to address 300 wary top management people in Paris. The president felt that his first task should be to give the French managers a comprehensive picture of the American company since they knew little about it.

The speech writer convinced him he should create a good cassette slide presentation of the corporate story in French. A French A-V firm produced the presentation, with a well-known French TV commentator as narrator, based on an English text supplied by the writer. The presentation was followed by the president's speech, a thoughtful 10-minute talk on the future of the partnership delivered in English using a translator.

The audience appreciated the fact the Americans had taken pains to present their corporate story in French with a familiar French voice. The president's earnest message at the conclusion was much better received than if the audience had first been made to endure 20 minutes of tedious translation of the U.S. company's history.

The translation of the speech was not a truly instant sight-reading of the text or translation of words as they were spoken. That approach puts the translator under terrific pressure.

Here are some suggestions to make translations effective:

Deliver copies of the text of the speech to the translators the day before the speech. Be available to answer questions, explain jargon, spell out nuances.

Have a news release translated and ready for distribution.

Encourage translators to emphasize key points. If you've watched U.N. proceedings on TV, you know translators' words are often delivered with as much passion as a plumbing instructor.

Hire only highly-skilled translators.

Prevail on the speaker to deliver the address slowly, with frequent pauses. Have the speech typed in a format that indicates places to pause and encourages a slow pace.

Avoid visual aids if possible (as part of the actual speech).

Keep in mind that the English language is unique for its brevity. Five words in English may require eight or nine in French or Spanish.

Make sure microphones, lines to translators' booths, and headsets are working before the speech starts. There is a whole new dimension of opportunities for electronic malfunction. Be prepared.

CONCLUSION

The work of at least some speech writers does not end until the moment the speaker walks up to the lectern. Then the writer, like the caddy when the golfer hits the ball in a big tournament, can only hope the speaker is in good form.

9

Delivering the Speech

Gentlemen, reading from speeches is a very tedious business, particularly for an old man who has to put on spectacles, and more so if the man be so tall that he has to bend over to the light.
—Abraham Lincoln, speech in Chicago (July 10, 1858)

Control of physical behavior is of vital importance to the speaker. The words alone will not get a message over to an audience. Audiences will respond to what speakers do as well as to what they say.

Much of the success of such speakers as Ronald Reagan, Lee Iacocca, and Mario Cuomo comes from the way they handle themselves as they deliver their speeches. The way they sound and the way they look helps to win over audiences—sometimes in spite of their speech content. These speakers use a manner of delivery that can best be described as earnest conversation. That approach best suits the expectations of a modern audience.

Most people judge a speaker's delivery on the basis of their everyday experiences with communication, where they commonly put as much or more weight on the how as on the what. When a parent asks a child, "Did you break this cup?" the words in the child's answer will get much less attention than the child's wavering eye movement, shifting posture, and unsteady tone of voice. Although listeners do not often articulate the standards of judgment they apply, they are most certainly affected by the way in which messages are delivered in both casual conversation and formal speeches.

Some people develop annoying habits that distract from their words. Nervous mannerisms, aimless motions, or monotonous vocal tone may replace ideas as the most powerful force in the speech. Yet large numbers of speakers have risen to important positions requiring a great deal of public speaking without having been told something as simple as "You really shouldn't scratch yourself *there* when giving a talk."

The emphasis should not all be on the negative. A speaker with ringing conviction in the voice can add a valuable dimension to the words on the page. Determination can be shown in facial expression, posture, and gesture far better than it can be stated in words. The presentation of the speech should not be considered a dull chore that must be done out of necessity; it is an opportunity to bring the ideas of a speech to life in the same way good news or strong convictions are expressed at home and in the office.

PRINCIPLES OF DELIVERY

Advice from the speech writer or a professional speech coach will give any speaker an impartial perspective on speech delivery that will help ensure that the speech will be presented to best advantage. But the speaker should realize that good coaching grows out of the application of the fundamental principles of effective speech delivery. These fundamentals, which should be understood by the speaker as well as the coach, can be reduced to a few simple but crucial points on proper management of voice and bodily action.

Contact with the Audience

Unless a speaker interacts with an audience, the message of the speech might just as well be delivered by tape recorder or even printed and mailed to its recipients. Eye contact between speaker and listener makes interaction possible. A speaker must look at—and see—the people in an audience if the feeling of a live presentation is to be preserved.

In conversation or in speaking from notes, a speaker has the valuable opportunity to adjust to audience responses: to add, to restate, to change direction. A speaker holding to the language of a manuscript lacks that flexibility but will nevertheless find eye contact beneficial—and a properly prepared script will help make eye contact possible.

Good eye contact will aid the speaker in holding attention. Listeners are less likely to talk to one another, to sleep, or to read a newspaper if the speaker periodically gets free of the text long enough to look at them. Eye contact will also give the speaker clues about how the delivery of the speech is progressing. Someone straining to hear, for example, makes it obvious that the speaker needs to get closer to the microphone or project the voice better. Signs of restlessness tell the speaker to move, gesture, or even pause to regain attention.

Often speakers will see signs of vigorous agreement or disagreement that tempt them to leave the safety of the manuscript and adjust the content of a speech in recognition of the response. Only highly skilled speakers can leave the page, add new material, and return to the manuscript smoothly. Most find it extremely difficult to make a logical transition back to the text, and should they do so successfully, the digression has added to the length of what was once a carefully timed speech. With thorough audience analysis, there should be relatively little need for digressions.

Although most speakers would be better off if they did not make significant alterations during delivery, some minor changes may prove useful. Occasionally a controversial passage may be marked to indicate the speaker should leave it in if the audience is responding well but take it out if the audience reacts negatively to earlier parts of the talk. And small asides, such as "I see Joe Jones agrees with that approach," may enliven a talk.

Eye contact must be real if it is to be of any value. Furtive glances at the back wall or blank looks at the spaces between listeners will not be helpful. With practice, almost any speaker can learn to pick up a sentence or a long phrase with a quick look and then deliver it directly to the audience.

The first line in the previous paragraph, for example, can be absorbed at a glance and then said without looking back down. That particular sentence would take about four seconds to deliver in normal speech. While it is being said, a speaker could establish meaningful eye contact with two people for two seconds each. By looking each person directly in the eye, the speaker could ensure their continued attention (or jolt them back into attention) and get a quick reading on how well the speech is being received.

In order to avoid making anyone feel uncomfortable, the speaker should not make just one or two people the targets of eye contact. A deliberate effort should be made to spread eye contact around, taking particular care to look at people in the back and on the far sides of the room. In a large audience, the speaker cannot look at everyone, but eye contact should be established with a representative sample of the audience.

One of the safest techniques for returning to the text after eye contact is also the simplest. The speaker looks a member of the audience directly in the eye, perhaps while gesturing forcefully with the left hand, and then picks up the next words at the point where the index finger of right hand has been firmly planted. Speakers who were broken of this habit in the first grade will be able to relearn it with a little practice.

A speaker should not wear a deadpan expression when making eye contact. Almost every speech has its light moments where a smile is appropriate, as well as its moments when a look of concern or alarm or satisfaction is in order. No speaker should be expected to take a short course in acting to show simple emotions through facial expression, but speakers should be reminded of the need to react normally in establishing eye contact. A speaker who habitually faces the public with a scowl (reflecting the speaker's discomfort rather than any ideas in the speech) may find it easier to use normal facial expressions when eye contact is made not with the lifeless manuscript but with live human beings in an audience.

Posture

A speaker normally needs a lectern to hold the manuscript, and even a speaker with access to an elaborate video prompting mechanism will usually be expected to stand half-hidden behind what will sometimes be a heavy mass of polished wood. If the speaker succumbs to the temptation to lean on or brace against the lectern, a barrier to communication will have been created.

Someone draped over a lectern does not present the image desired in a speech where a speaker addresses important issues and offers vital information. The posture of a speaker unable to stand up without suport suggests uncertainty and unsteadiness. While audiences are seldom conscious of the details of posture, a speaker twisted into a pretzel position will send a subtle, nonverbal message that subconsciously advises the listener not to take the speaker seriously.

The speaker should stand free and clear of the lectern, with weight balanced almost equally on each foot. Speakers should aim for a posture of relaxed attention. The shoulders should be level. Without being excessively rigid, the back should be straight and the head up. This posture projects an image that is square, solid, and alert—an image appropriate for the messages most speakers want to deliver.

Gesture

Many people are self-conscious and even embarrassed about their gestures. "People tell me I talk with my hands" seems almost a confession of guilt. In fact, gestures are helpful in communication. They serve a variety of useful functions.

Gestures emphasize. The thrusting index finger may be the most common emphatic gesture, but a number of movements from the two-handed chopping motion to the pounding of the fist help a speaker signal, "Now hear this; this idea is important."

Gestures describe. Movement of the hands can show direction, size, and shape. When speakers talk of something large or small, fast or slow, up or down, or straight or crooked, gestures naturally supplement the words of the speech.

Gestures signal. From the obvious use of a "thumps up" or "we're number one" to the more subtle open-handed gesture accompanying a plea for help, many gestures have acquired a generally accepted meaning in a given society.

Gestures relieve tension. Most speakers feel more at ease after they have made a few gestures. The movement expends some of the pent-up nervousness that goes along with speaking.

Gestures attract attention. A motionless speaker usually has little more appeal to the eye than any other lifeless object before the audience. The motion of a gesture can attract the attention of an audience.

Preplanned or canned gestures almost always look odd because the timing is usually off. A gesture ordinarily comes at the very moment an idea is being emphasized, described, or otherwise supported by a gesture. It may precede the idea slightly in some cases. Canned gestures tend to come a split second late, and they almost always appear ludicrous. Speakers should attempt in rehearsal of a talk to find places where a gesture feels natural rather than arbitrarily to insert a few where the writer thinks the speech needs some help.

Many speakers who gesture with vigor in normal conversation will make tiny motions while speaking. These motions cannot be seen by most listeners, and if they are seen, they appear quite out of place. Speakers should be aware of the need to get gestures free of the lectern so they will not be blocked from the audience's view.

It can be amusing to watch a speaker search for places to bring hands to rest when they are not in motion. The lectern is sometimes gripped tightly, or the hands may travel about the body searching for a landing place. To the amusement of some in an audience, a speaker may resort to the fig leaf positon, with hands clasped at arms length in front of the body.

There are three comfortable positions for hands when they are not performing some useful service such as gesturing or turning a page. They may hang normally at the sides. Many speakers find this feels odd at first, and they need to be reassured that it looks normal. There is nothing wrong with one or both hands in the pockets if the result is casual and not strained—and if the pockets allow for the hands to fit comfortably. Or hands may rest lightly on the lectern. So long as the speaker does not put any weight on them or cling to the sides of the stand with them, this arrangement places the hands in a convenient place from which to launch a gesture.

Voice

In earnest conversation most people use their voices effectively without thinking about it. Some problems often develop in formal speaking, however, and they deserve attention.

The Drone. Monotony in voice results from excessive regularity in pitch and rate. The solution does not come from speakers' attempting to manipulate the melody and or alternate the speed of the voice. This would quite likely produce an odd singsong effect as bad as the original problem. A speaker can develop a more lively voice by thinking of the speech not as a sequence of words but as a sequence of ideas. Arranging and marking the phrases on the page may make it easier to break up excessive monotony by putting the speaker's focus on the clusters of meaningful phrases.

The Racer. Many speakers speed up when they think a speech is going badly. The usual result is to make the speech even worse than the speaker thought it was. The suggestion to slow down is a rather simple one compared to the complicated manipulations of the voice required in avoiding monotony. Therefore most speakers are able to monitor their rate and reduce it once the problem comes to their attention.

In addition to slowing the number of words per minute in a passage, a speaker can take advantage of the pause. Some speakers will find that including the instructions "(Pause)" in the manuscript at appropriate places will help. The best solution in most cases would be for the speaker to mark up the manuscript using double or triple slash marks to indicate pauses of various lengths. At no point, however, should the process become mechanical.

The Pontificator. The speaker, faced with a microphone or an audience, naturally may feel that the normal speaking voice is not impressive enough. But speakers should avoid trying for an abnormally low pitch and an impressive but strained vocal quality. Large numbers of people do not like the sounds of their own voices, but except in extraordinary cases, audiences soon adjust to the sound of the speaker. Therefore speakers should not attempt to mimic the vocal timbre of professional actors or announcers. Such an effort will produce strain along with an artificiality that can distract listeners.

The Inaudible. When a microphone is required so that the speaker can be heard, it should have already been properly adjusted before the speaker begins. The speaker should speak not to the mike but through it to the audience. Depending on the capability of the equipment, the speaker's movement in the delivery of the speech may be severely limited.

If possible, a microphone should not be used. A speaker should be advised to project or aim the voice at the farthest person in the room. It is usually not a good idea for a speaker to think of talking louder. This advice may result in strain.

GUIDELINES FOR HANDLING VISUAL AIDS

Many of the problems speakers encounter with visual aids can be solved by careful preparation of the material. Part of the successful use of visuals, however, depends on the speaker's performance in delivery. An excellent visual can be distracting if not used properly.

First, speakers should not gaze at the aid. Few sights are more ludicrous than an adult standing in front of an audience while engaged in a serious discussion with a chart on an easel or a slide on a screen. When the speech writer has prepared the aids correctly, the speaker has the right to expect the charts to be in order and the right picture to appear on the screen at the proper time. Only an occasional quick glance will be required to tell the speaker if everything is in order. Beyond that, there can be little justification for the speaker to stare at the aid.

Second, the visual aid should be in view only at the point in a speech where it helps the audience understand the speaker's idea. An attractive visual brought up in advance will almost always deflect attention away from the speaker. Ideally aids should be removed as soon as they are no longer needed, but audiences are usually not as likely to be distracted by an aid after it has been used as they are if it is presented before it is needed.

CONCLUSION

No one should fall for the mistaken belief that good speakers are born, not made. With a little attention to the basics of good delivery, any speaker can make more effective use of those features of voice and action that almost everyone uses in earnest conversation.

10

Writing Speeches of Courtesy, Slide Talks, and Presentations

We cannot complete any public building or monument only with stone and mortar. It is never completed until the speeches are made.
—Brigance (1961, 490)

When a typical building project has been completed, a number of speeches will have played a part in the total process. There are the dedication speeches, of course, and before that a variety of specialized talks, not public speeches in the ordinary sense of the term, were needed to keep everyone informed and to win approval for various phrases of the operation. And the standard public talk that has been the primary concern of this book until now also carried part of the communication load. But three special kinds of speeches have not yet been examined: the speech of courtesy, the slide talk, and the presentation.

THE SPEECH OF COURTESY

Not all speeches are major addresses dealing with burning issues. Speakers, as William Norwood Brigance points out, "will often have to perform appropriate acts of courtesy on public occasions—introduce a speaker, welcome a guest, present a gift or an award, etc. Custom requires you to say something" (Brigance 1961, 491).

Almost any corporation or other organization has its equivalent of the White House's "Rose Garden rubbish." Former presidential speech writer John B. McDonald reviewed the 1972 *Public Papers of the Presidents* and counted, along with 432 major texts, 420 additional White House releases, 346 additional White House announcements, 78 proclamations, 55 executive orders, 65 presidential reports to Congress, and 15 other miscellaneous presidential documents. The president needed appropriate remarks for proclamations on National Beta Club Week, National Check Your Vehicle Emissions Month, and National Coaches Day. He required remarks on the Great Lakes Basin Commission, the Swan Island Treaty, and the official position on procedures for use of off-road vehicles on public lands (McDonald 1977, A 11).

Special types of speeches have a number of characteristics that set them off from the standard public speech. They usually are short. They have a streamlined structure with little attention ordinarily paid to making major points or divisions of the talk emerge clearly; more attention is paid to subtle transitions. These speeches almost always have a friendly, social tone. They have little concern with proof or evidence. And they can be less conversational in language, almost to the point of being literary in some instances.

The special types examined here are the speech of introduction, the speech of award or tribute, the dedication speech, the commencement address, and the speech to entertain.

Speech of Introduction

The speech of introduction requires that three basic pieces of information be communicated to the audience: the speaker's name, the speaker's qualifications to talk on the topic, and the title or subject matter of the speech. This informaton should be conveyed in less than three minutes, with one to two minutes being a good range.

Most of the advice for constructing a good speech of introduction can best be phrased in the negative.

Don't overdo it. The speech of introduction should be low key. In delivery and content, it should not be so dynamic that it becomes a hard act for the speaker to follow. Extravagant praise of the speaker should be avoided. Speeches of introduction should not promise an audience the speaker will be great. If the speaker does prove to be good, the audience can decide for itself. The introduction should merely serve to help make it clear to the audience that the speaker is qualified to speak. Even the humor should not be too good. If the introducer gets gales of laughter, the speaker's opening humor may appear weak by comparison.

Don't use clichés. Avoid such phrases as "A speaker who needs no introduction," "Without further ado," "It is a high privilege and a distinct honor," and "I am happy to present." Commonsense substitutions can be used: "Many of us have known our speaker during the ten years he has managed the Ajax plant in Centerville," "I know we are all interested in hearing what Bob has to say," and "I'm glad we were finally able to work out a time when our speaker could appear on one of our programs."

Don't preempt the speaker's topic. A speech of introduction that discusses the speaker's topic runs the risk of either taking away one of the speaker's ideas or, worse, contradicting the speaker. References to the speaker's subject should be limited to its significance or timeliness.

Don't include a false ending. The good speech of introduction has a rhythm that builds to the point when the speaker stands and advances to the lectern with the applause of the audience welling up in greeting. If the speaker thinks the introduction has ended and starts to rise, only to discover there is more to come, the experience can be unnerving. Although the speech of introduction may conclude with the speaker's topic, the safest way of ending finishes with the speaker's name: "Here, then, to give us a successful manager's perspective on that topic—Jane Jackson."

Don't count on inspiration. The speech of introduction should be written out in full and read without ad libs. Speaking from notes or memory in introducing a speaker can be a disaster. Introducers have been known to forget the name of the speaker. They often blurt out inane comments. And they can easily make errors in word choice of the sort that occurred when a presiding officer tried to thank a guest for filling in at the last minute by saying, "As most of you know, we weren't able to get the speaker we really wanted tonight."

Don't read a vita. A simple autobiographical data sheet can become a dangerous tool in the hands of some program organizers. They will read an entire three-page vita of a speaker or will select arbitrary, ill-chosen segments for an introduction. A good rule is for the writer to prepare a speech of introduction for the use of the person who has the responsibility of introducing the speaker. This speech can usually be written double spaced on a single page in vita form. To avoid possible offense, it should not be identified as a speech of introduction but can be labeled, "Background information on Mr. Jones for his address to the Town Club on January 12."

The introduction writers prepare for their own speakers to deliver in introducing other speakers may be somewhat more elaborate than the bare bones type limited to a single page. The longer introduction allows for personal comments on the qualification of the speaker, for example, although these comments should not extend to promising that the speech will be good. This style of introduction can be somewhat more elevated in language than the other.

The following sample is taken from the last paragraph of an introduction written in the vita style followed by a sample of the personal style:

[Vita style:] Mr. Price joined Wellhead Oil in 1970 as director of corporate writing. He has supervised the departments of internal and external communication and was responsible for the creation of the award-winning employee magazine, *Gush*. Mr. Price's topic for discussion in his appearance in Midtown is "Speaking Up and Speaking Out."

[Personal style:] For more than ten years Tom Price has directed a dynamic communication program at Wellhead Oil. He has helped make Wellhead an industry leader in addressing public issues. And Tom has recognized the crucial role of internal communications. He created Wellhead's employee publication, *Gush*, which in the past eight years has won three Silver Key awards—quite a record! To address us on the topic "Speaking Up and Speaking Out," we could not have found a better qualified communicator than . . . Mr. Thomas V. Price.

Speech of Award or Tribute

Service awards, retirements, speaker bureau activity citations, prize-winning suggestions—these and many more occasions require a speech of tribute. Such a speech can be built on three principles: pour on the praise, back it up with a concrete example, and include a personal note from the speaker.

The praise in an award situation can hardly be too heavy. If an employee is being rewarded for saving a thousand dollars with a suggestion on the assembly line, that thousand dollars can be multiplied by the number of employees in the company to show how much the contribution of an individual can mean. Whatever courage, brains, effort, or endurance has been demonstrated should be extolled in the warmest terms.

The accomplishment of the individual must be made concrete. The speech cannot possibly fit any other individual. If a prize-winning suggestion was made by someone on the job for only a year, that can be the hook on which to hang the talk. If the speaker bureau member had to drive through a snowstorm to give a talk in order to become eligible for an award, that can be mentioned.

The speaker must make the presentation personal. The speaker who has no way at all of knowing the person should at least arrange for information to get to the speaker from a supervisor so the speaker can say, "In discussing the person we honor here today, the plant manager told me. . . ."

When several people are to be recognized for an award, every winner's name should be mentioned and the awards presented individually. This may call for some ingenuity in finding ways to say "the next winner is . . ." but the temptation to handle the winners in groups will deprive them of their moment in the spotlight.

The retirement speech generally has a touch of humor, as do some of the other award speeches. In such situations, humor serves to take the edge off the embarrassment the speaker or the award recipient might feel. Humor should not be considered mandatory, however. Unless both speaker and recipient are comfortable with it, it will not work. Friendliness and warmth will accomplish the required ends as well as humor does.

Dedication Speech

Speeches marking the refurbishing and reopening of the Statue of Liberty on the Fourth of July in 1986 were a key part of that special national celebration. Although most other dedications are at a much lower level of importance and excitement, they all require appropriate prepared remarks.

Several themes work well in the dedication speech. First, from both a practical and a symbolic point of view, the use of a new plant or a new project can be discussed. Second, the individuals who planned and constructed the plant or project can be praised. And, third, the future impact of the new facility can be explored.

Commencement Speech

A commencement speech can be a slightly altered version of the ordinary public speech discussed in previous chapters. A speaker representing a particular industry, for example, might make a speech on the future of the country from the perspective of that industry. With a few topical references to the occasion, the speech would meet the demands of the situation.

Many commencement speeches are much more ceremonial in nature. They address broad and abstract themes. For better or worse, most of them are promptly forgotten if they are listened to at all.

The speaker's job is to present a talk that does not violate the spirit of the occasion. The topic should almost never be controversial. Graduates feel a great sense of release from authority on commencement day and are prone to express themselves rudely if they find they have to endure an extra lecture.

The spirit of the occasion will be violated by a speech that is too long. Fifteen minutes marks the outer limits, but too much under ten minutes of speaking may not appear to do justice to the invitation. Rarely will a commencement speaker find it advisable to refer to the length of the speech. A promise to keep the remarks short may draw applause and will tend to denigrate the speaker's effort. A pithy twelve minutes will be appreciated without any effort on the part of the speaker to brag on the brevity of the address.

The essentials of the commencement address may be characterized somewhat casually as note, gloat, quote, and float.

First, the speech must take *note* of all the people involved in the occasion. No matter how repetitious it may sound to someone who attends graduations frequently, the parents of the graduates should be credited for their contribution to the successful completion of schooling. So should the administration of the school and the faculty. A kind word for alumni and donors would not be out of order. And, of course, the graduating class must be recognized for its accomplishment.

Second, hyperbole has its place in a commencement address. The speaker should *gloat* in the sense of the term that means to gaze with admiration and affection. The honor of the invitation to speak can be mentioned, though such invitations are at times not too subtle hints for a contribution to the school or an effort to borrow the speaker's prestige for a school that needs its reputation polished. The school itself should be praised for whatever accomplishments the writer can dig up. The city, the state, the founders, the library, the athletic program, or anything else that has any worth at all can be subjects for praise.

Third, the speech can have a faint scholarly or literary ring. A *quote* or two of suitable merit can be included by a speaker who in other situations might not be inclined to use such material. The text of the speech itself can be a bit more literary than usual. More attention can be paid to alliteration, balance, rhythm, climax, and rhetorical questions than would be the case if the speaker were addressing a civic club at a noon meeting.

Fourth, the speech can *float* a vision of the future. This standard theme of the commencement address requires the speaker to assert that the future is bright or challenging or dangerous or wonderful. The speech might contain a few helpful suggestions on getting the most from the future or avoiding its pitfalls. The speaker's experience and reputation can be cited here to bolster modest suggestions for success.

In recent years students who have had a voice in selecting commencement speakers have shown a preference for celebrities and for entertaining speeches. A humorous speech of the sort that Art Buchwald might give would be well received, but humor of that quality is hard to produce and hard to deliver. If a speaker has a flair for light material, however, this possibility should not be overlooked.

Speech to Entertain

Only rarely are speakers called on to give purely entertaining speeches. The principal types of speeches in which humor is the end and not a means are the presentation at a roast and the after-dinner speech.

The Roast. The roast speech is perhaps the more difficult of the two. The fine art of the humorous insult requires a deft touch. The essence of the roast gibe is that it must be broad enough to be unreal and true enough to fit the character of the person who is the butt of the humor. The subject matter of the jokes should be something that in some way can be seen as a virtue. Even Dean Martin's drinking, apart from its value in giving Martin a ready means of audience identification, has its positive aspects because of the implied compliment in the "what a great drinker he is" message.

All of these characteristics are seen in a joke President Reagan made at a dinner honoring Bob Hope. It was not true, Mr. Reagan claimed, that Hope entertained the troops at Yorktown; he was at Valley Forge. The gibe fits Bob Hope as a dedicated USO entertainer, and it teases him about his age (read "durabilty") as an implicit virtue.

On the other hand, when President Carter in a different roast situation said that Governor Jerry Brown was California's way of celebrating the International Year of the Child, the humor was not well received. The exaggeration was not broad enough to fall outside the range of what Mr. Carter might have said in earnest; the bite of the joke was too sharp.

The After-Dinner Speech. Some speeches after dinner are not intended to be funny. They may use a small amount of humor but are simply regular speeches that happen to be given after a meal. The speech under consideration here, the humorous after-dinner speech, is one that has entertainment as its major objective. The after-dinner speech does have a message; if it did not, it would no longer be a speech but a comedy routine. The message, however, remains subordinate to the humor.

The message can be tacked on at the end of the speech—a fairly common practice with after-dinner speeches having an inspirational theme—or the theme of the speech can be loosely supported by the humor.

Apart from deciding where the message will appear, the after-dinner speech has little structure other than a string of humorous bits. The tried and true pieces of humor should be spread out somewhat to ensure that all the laughter does not come in one short segment of the speech, but the pattern of organization can be highly flexible.

A speech on the topic of consumer service presented at an awards banquet for a group of utility employees might consist of a series of stories about problems with consumers. Anecdotes can be cited and excerpts from letters read. The speech can be padded with material on consumers and human relations gathered from standard sources of humor. The speech can end with a few comments on the difficulty of working with customers and the importance of seeing the lighter side of the job.

An inspirational humorous speech can be developed on the subject of sales. Anecdotes, one-liners, and quotations on selling can lead to a brief motivational passage on the importance of sales and the sales force. The shift from the humorous to the inspirational is possible because the humor creates an emotional response in the audience and the conclusion of the speech keeps the emotional pitch high but redirects it to a new channel.

No speech writer should be expected to have the ability to write humor at the level of a professional comedy writer. For very important speeches, then, it may be wise to invest in the services of a specialist. Writing a successful joke is a difficult task, one at which few writers have had the opportunity to gain experience.

Summary

From Lincoln's Gettysburg Address to the most recent inaugural speech by a U.S. president, ceremonial speeches of courtesy have played a significant role in the history of speech making. Even more than most other speeches, these special types of addresses must fit the circumstances in which they are given. More important than their content is their style and their tone.

Lincoln's suggestion at Gettysburg that "the world will little note nor long remember what we say here" was not true for the spirit of his speech. It would have been accurate for the substance of his address had he not sounded the right note of appropriate eloquence. His observation was fully accurate for the excellent oration by Edward Everett that preceded Lincoln's speech. Most people do not even remember the name of the other speaker at Gettysburg—the one who spoke for two hours.

SLIDE TALK

The word *speech* has been used in this book so far in reference to a talk in which an audience would be asked to focus its full attention on a speaker delivering a message in person. Implicitly, any visuals used in such a talk would be aids that would play a subordinate role.

Visuals may command a much more prominent position in some kinds of communication. In a multimedia show or a movie, the entire message will be carried by a mechanical AV medium with considerable attention to music and even sound effects, as well as the human voice. If a speaker is featured at all, the speaker's performance has been captured on videotape or audiotape.

The slide talk falls somewhere between the ordinary public speech and the film or video show in blending prepared visual aids in with the voice of a speaker who provides a live—or sometimes taped—narration. The dividing line between a public speech and a slide talk, then, has been crossed when the audience focuses its attention at least as much on the slides as on the speaker. A good slide talk should not keep a slide on the screen for more than ten seconds. In such a fast-paced visual show, the live speaker is reduced to little more than a "talking head" in the corner of the room. In fact, the speaker's voice may be taped so that the live element will be removed altogether.

Slide talks have special value in presenting technical information or showing how something works. Abstract topics can be presented as well. Various subjects covered in this book could readily be made into slide talks: "The History of Speech Writing," "The Speaker-Writer Relationship," and "Humor in Speech Writing."

Once a script and its accompanying slides have been prepared, delivery of the talk can be quickly mastered. If necessary, several speakers can soon be dispatched to spread the message to a number of audiences.

Much of the talent required to write a public speech has its application in writing slide talks. Good oral style and most of the other guidelines for language will apply. Audience analysis and determining the purpose of the talk also should figure in the planning stages of a slide talk. Although the slide talk may follow some of the guidelines for organizing a public speech, a simple narration or other variations will often be appropriate alternatives.

Detailed information on the writing of a slide talk may be found in the Bibliography. Only a brief summary will be offered here of the steps to follow before the writing of the final script.

An early determination should be made of the intended purpose of the talk by considering its impact on the audience or audiences to whom it will be shown. An outline of ideas to be included in the script should be prepared and appropriate pictures indicated for each idea. At least six slides per minute of presentation will be required, and a 3 x 5 or 5 x 8 card should be used to represent each proposed picture. These planning cards should have penciled in a rough sketch of the visual, a production note giving any details such as camera angle or perspective to be used in taking any photographs that may be required, comments on the text that will be supported by the visual, and a consecutive number for the card.

The cards can be displayed on a wall, a table, or a planning board to see them in sequence. Then the script can be written and any sound effects indicated. The script should provide cues to show where the speaker is to change slides. Only after a rough draft of the script has been completed should an investment be made in slides.

THE PRESENTATION

Another special kind of speech is the presentation. Like the word *speech*, the term *presentation* can be applied rather loosely to a number of different kinds of talks. No precise definition has been agreed on, but in general a presentation typically has a cluster of characteristics that separate it from the standard public speech.

The set of characteristics listed below usually but not always delineates the presentation as a special kind of speech. When most of these characteristics are present, a writer should recognize that the talk being prepared differs from a normal speech. Special adaptation will then be required.

Special Features

Audience. The audience for a presentation frequently has two characteristics that are not typical for the standard public speech. First, the audience may be smaller than that for the usual speech. A presentation may be given to a single person in a situation where a speech in the normal sense of the word would be unthinkable. A proposal from the head of the speech writing department to the head of the communications department asking for authorization to hire an additional writer might be made as an oral presentation, even though it could be accompanied by or followed by a written request. Presentations often have for an audience a committee or a board consisting of only a handful of listeners. Like all of the other characteristics of presentations, exceptions will be found where a presentation will be delivered to an audience of hundreds.

Second, the audience tends to be made up of decision makers who have the power to approve or disapprove of any request made in the presentation. Many presentations have as their object the selling of a product, service, or idea. A proposal offered to a corporate board of directors, for example, depends for its success on the board's approval, which may be given or denied almost immediately after the delivery of the presentation.

Several implications arise for the writer from the nature of the typical audience for a presentation. Adaptation may be much more precise than for a regular speech. Individual idiosyncrasies may be precisely taken into account, as in the case of a member of the audience who is known to have passion for precise cost estimates or a strong aversion to new ideas. In some cases, one or two listeners in the audience have the real power; the presentation may be directed almost exclusively to this minority. Because a decision will usually be required, special care must be given to the action step in a presentation.

Dealing with Questions. While a public speaker would be disturbed if interrupted by questions during the speech, such interruptions are normal and even helpful in a presentation. To a large degree, this difference grows out of the nature of the audience for a presentation; they are decision makers listening to someone who is probably a subordinate in an organization, and they have no reason to feel reluctant about injecting questions whenever they wish.

Such questions will ordinarily be helpful to the person making a presentation because, in addition to supplying any specific information a questioner needs, the questions can help build a bond between speaker and audience as they work toward a decision together. Possible questions can be anticipated; in addition, the script should include places where they are called for.

Use of Visuals. Speeches may employ visual aids; presentations almost always do. Also, unlike speeches, handouts may be distributed during a presentation. Many types of aids unsuitable for speeches, such as a small model of a proposed building or samples of paper stock to be used in a publication, may be used to good effect. Standard charts and slides also have a place.

The writer must use somewhat great ingenuity in preparing visuals for a presentation and must write the script to allow for pauses in dealing with handouts or models and to make special efforts to refocus attention on the script after distractions caused by a hands-on aid. The writer may violate the usual rule that calls for the words of a speech manuscript never to refer to the visuals. A presentation may include such statements as, "You can see in the floor diagram . . ." and "The figures in the right-hand column of the blue sheet. . . ."

Length. Again remembering that the characteristics of a presentation described here are usually but not always present, it should be noted that presentations are frequently longer than speeches. In spite of the fact that the topic of a presentation will often be more narrowly focused than a speech ("We need a new format for the company magazine" as opposed to "Employee communications serve modern business well"), the wealth of detail in a presentation requires more time to develop. Where the typical speech runs about twenty minutes, a presentation more commonly takes forty-five minutes or an hour to deliver.

A writer must recognize the demands on a listener's attention span when a script lasts for more than half an hour and attempt to make the style and content as lively as possible.

Team Delivery. Unlike a normal speech, a presentation may be delivered by two or more persons. This approach permits experts on more than one aspect of the subject to be involved, and it adds variety that helps compensate for a presentation's length.

Writing for a team has several implications for the writer. As a rule, frequent shifts from one speaker to the other will add more interest than, say, giving two speakers thirty minutes each in an hour-long presentation. Special attention must be paid in the script to appropriate style and content for each person. More rehearsal may be required to coordinate the work of several speakers, with special emphasis on the use of visual aids. Also, each member of the team needs to be drilled in the importance of demonstrating an intense interest in what other members of the team have to say during the presentation.

Organizing the Ideas

The presentation, like the speech of courtesy and the slide talk, may not always follow the standard organizational pattern for public speeches. One of the possible variations calls for moving through six steps: (1) a business-like opening, (2) background information, (3) relevant criteria, (4) the proposal, (5) justification of the proposal, and (6) the desired action.

A Business-like Opening. In making a presentation, a speaker cannot always count on being introduced to the audience. It may be necessary for the speaker to walk boldly to the front of the room and begin. Even when the speaker is introduced, that introduction often lacks the social overtones found in being welcomed to the Rotary Club. As a rule, then, a presentation begins on a more business-like note than a normal speech. The use of the common bond, the compliment, the story, and the touch of humor may be out of place.

The listeners need to know who is speaking and what organization or department the speaker represents. They need to know the general subject matter that will be dealt with in the presentation. They do not, however, need to be told precisely what the speaker will be asking for. A request for six new word processors, for example, should be referred to as a "discussion of equipment needs in the communications office."

If this information on who is speaking, from where, and on what has not been supplied in advance, the speaker should give it concisely. If it has been supplied, the speaker's opening needs to consist of little more than "Good morning" or "Good afternoon."

Background Information. A quick summary of events leading up to the presentation serves two purposes. First, it makes sure that attention is devoted to the proper issue. The speaker may be one of several individuals giving presentations, and some listeners may not know exactly where they are on their agenda. It should be remembered that the listeners are usually in the middle of their business day; they have left work on their desks only minutes before in some cases, and their attention may be there instead of on the speaker's subject.

Second, background information can eliminate a great deal of wasted effort by bringing listeners up to date on what has already been decided. If the president has already approved the concept of a new fleet of trucks, the listeners need to be reminded of this so they can devote their attention not to reopening old questions but to deciding on which make of vehicle to buy.

Criteria. The way to a favorable decision can be paved by establishing clearly the standards that all agree a proposal should meet to be adopted. A speaker making a pitch for a new project may say, "I know that you have three questions in mind when we add a new product to the line. Is it consistent with what we now offer? Can we produce it with the quality that our reputation demands? And can we begin to turn a profit within a reasonable length of time?" If these are indeed the criteria the group applies to new products, the speaker has the proper issues in focus before wasting any time talking about the product itself or what action the group is being asked to take.

Common criteria include such areas as cost or feasibility, but the criteria should be based on the particular case. Cost may be of no concern in a crash program, and in another, highly specialized criteria may apply.

The Proposal. Once the standards used to evaluate an idea are established, the essence of the speaker's proposal should be presented. Now is the time for, "We need six Model Zip word processors before work starts on the annual report." The action called for should not usually be revealed at this time. Enough detail should be presented, however, for the proposal to be evaluated fairly in the next step. It should be made clear if new funds are required, if a shift in a budget line is being asked for, or if the speaker wants to divert six machines from the accounting department.

Justification. With the proposal clearly set forth, the speaker needs to show that it meets the criteria established in the third step. In the case of the example of proposing a new product, the presentation should demonstrate that the product is consistent with the company line, it is a high-quality item, and it can be expected to be profitable in two years.

The justification step should show that all the criteria can be met or offer an explanation of why any one of them should be set aside. In addition, the speaker should include in the justification any bonus points that show the idea has advantages over and above what would normally be expected.

Action. The final step deals with what the decision makers need to do to implement the proposal. Actions may include voting, authorizing, forwarding to the next level of authority, or delegating responsibility. A properly prepared action step takes into account what the listeners have the power to do and calls for the specific act that will get the results desired. Using the example of the word processors, a distinction may be made between the topic of the presentation and the proposal as well as between the proposal and the action step. The topic is the new equipment request; the proposal is that the department needs six Model Zip word processors; the action is that the committee votes to add $15,000 to the department's equipment budget.

The organizational scheme outlined here will probably be a bit too mechanical for most proposals in ordinary speeches. But its systematic build toward gaining approval from decision makers makes it well suited for possible use in constructing a presentation.

CONCLUSION

Between the time someone gets the idea for building a new plant and the time the governor cuts the ribbon in the parking lot, a writer may have an opportunity to write one or more of all of the special types of speeches discussed here. They serve a number of valuable purposes, and they require the same planning and hard work needed for the standard public speech.

11

Making the Most of Speeches in the Communications Program

Finally—and perhaps most importantly—the chief executive in the year 2000 will have a personal responsibility for advocacy, activism and out-spokenness. Increasingly, the CEO will be expected to represent articulately and coherently his company and industry to their critics.
—David Rockefeller, "The Chief Executive in the Year 2000," *Vital Speeches* (January 1, 1980)

In 1924 when he created the character Babbitt, novelist Sinclair Lewis gave the world a crude stereotype of the American businessman. Nowhere was the Lewis characterization more biting than in his picture of George Babbitt as a public speaker. The image of Babbitt that Lewis left in the American mind was that of a mindless establishment booster whose speeches echoed the empty rhetoric of the ads he wrote for his real estate firm.

Ridicule of Babbitt's interest in public speaking and scorn for the recognition he gained with his oratory permeate the novel. Lewis lashed out at speech making in all its forms. He introduced such unsavory characters as the Reverend Dr. John Jennison Drew whose aimless alliteration impressed Babbitt for what he mistook as "thought and culture." There was also the sophistical Professor Joseph K. Pumphrey who owned something called the Riteway Business College where he taught public speaking among his many subjects.

As a novelist, Lewis had no artistic obligation to be fair or accurate regarding public speaking in the business world. His novel's success, however, caused the element of bombast on which he based his exaggerated descriptions to gain wide public acceptance as the essence of business speaking.

Anyone who wishes to give serious consideration to the role of speeches in any organization's communication program should be aware that the negative attitudes expressed about speech by Sinclair Lewis have appeared repeatedly throughout history. For centuries, the demise of public speaking as a significant form of communication has been predicted. Plato believed that philosophy, with its logical and methodical search for ultimate truth, would eliminate the need for speeches. When the printing press came along, it no longer seemed necessary to gather audiences for a message that could be printed in mass quantities and distributed to be read at leisure. Then came radio and television.

But public speaking endures. It remains a simple and effective means of communication. And it has become, in the Western world at least, part of our social fabric. What politician would dare run for office on only the strength of skillfully produced commercials and ads? What minister would be content to trust in sensitivity groups to replace the message from the pulpit?

Business speaking, a product of the twentieth century, shows steady growth. The increase in corporate speaking occurs at the same time companies are making excellent use of media unheard of a few decades ago. Closed circuit television supplements the old-fashioned bulletin board. Employee publications have the professional touch of the best national news magazines. Multimedia presentations rival the dramatic power of the movie screen. The parallel growth of speaking with the newer media of communication can be found not only in corporations but in nonprofit organizations, government agencies, and the professions as well.

A STRATEGY FOR SPEAKING

Partly as a result of the assumption that speeches are delivered on demand, an organization may not have a conscious strategy for using speech as a medium of communication. Often speech writers do not even help to determine which speaking invitations should be accepted. And the program is often passive rather than proactive.

No organization should feel it necessary to wait for invitations to speak or for occasions where a speech is required by circumstances. Invitations may be solicited subtly or directly. Employees may be asked to generate requests for speeches from groups they belong to. Direct approaches may be made to officers in charge of programs. Any company officer who serves on the directing body of a community organization with the president of a university has the chance to make known a willingness to speak to students. Brochures may be mailed making the availability of speakers known.

Any successful organization with a marketing program knows its market. But all too often a corporation with a desperate need to communicate does not have a clear notion of target audiences for speeches.

A list of desired audiences could be drawn up. It might give attention to hostile groups or disinterested audiences the company needs to reach. A clear policy should be stated in regard to school groups. Are major efforts in responding to elementary schools' requests for speakers in the company's best interest, or is the company merely making the day easier for teachers? Does the company need to reach college groups? If so, is the message to be aimed at business students, at liberal arts classes, or at some other segment of the population?

Maybe too many speeches are being given to audiences that do not need the message. Any corporation that devotes all of its speaking efforts to "hooray for private enterprise" talks before civic club audiences should question the value of a program that does little more than tell people what they already know and believe.

The prestige of audiences must be weighted. One talk to a group of opinion leaders may be worth dozens of speeches to lesser groups. Some audiences give the speaker a hearing beyond the confines of company or community. If an organization has a speaker who aspires to be viewed as an industry leader, speeches will be one avenue to that goal.

A balance should be planned among employee, public, and industry-professional audiences. The division need not be even, but it should represent the organization's communication needs and not some chance or arbitrary expenditure of time and energy.

A frank assessment should be made of the abilities of available speakers. Their strong and weak points should be considered in planning the best way to use each person. Care must be taken not to overburden good speakers or the top officials in an organization. Almost routinely requests for speakers will be for the highest-ranking person in the field, but acceding to such requests may not always be the best course of action. A tier system might be considered, with one set of objectives for the highest-ranking officers and another for a level of speakers taken from middle management.

The considerations cited here do not exhaust the possible concerns that should enter into the planning of a speech communication strategy. They do, however, suggest some of the reasons communication through speeches should not be left to chance.

THE SPEAKERS' BUREAU

A speakers' bureau offers an excellent way to harness the speaking power of an organization. A bureau can reach a surprising number of people. If, for example, an organization had fifty speakers giving two speeches a month, they would reach 1,200 audiences in a year. With an average of only forty people in an audience, 48,000 listeners would get the message or messages the bureau wanted to deliver. Each message could be tailored to fit the needs of the particular segment of the mass audience being addressed.

Bureau Support

For a speakers' bureau to work, it must have top management support. The outlay required in time, energy, and money is too great to sustain without backing from management in the form of budget and prestige.

A speakers' bureau cannot be grafted onto a full-blown communications program. It demands more than a few extra hours a month from a secretary and a director. Unless some other program is being phased out or downgraded, additional personnel will be needed to run a bureau properly. Speakers' bureaus often succeed better than expected. Legitimate requests for speakers may soon tax the ability of the bureau to train speakers, process invitations to speak, and keep the extensive records a well managed bureau should have. There must be an adequate budget to sustain this level of activity.

The prestige factor may determine whether a bureau begins its life in a healthy state. With a few encouraging words from top officials, the better candidates for the bureau are likely to emerge. Also, the supervisors of the speakers will be more cooperative if the bureau has warm approval at the highest levels. Supervisors can have a negative influence on the desire of speakers to volunteer. A few cool remarks from a boss can dampen the ardor of a speaker who otherwise might be an active member of the bureau.

Objectives

A speakers' bureau should have clear goals that are consistent with the overall objective of an organization's total speaking program. Bureaus that have been in existence for a number of years may lose sight of their reason for being. No less often than once a year, a bureau director should restate and reassess bureau aims.

In spite of the danger of wandering away from its original path, a bureau's flexibility can be a virtue. If communication goals change, the bureau can change. If a problem arises suddenly and needs to be addressed, the bureau can be the medium to accomplish the task.

A brief review of the basic ends of a single speech—to inform, to stir feelings, to change minds, and to get action—can provide a framework for analysis of the objections of an entire bureau. Like any one speech, a bureau must be designed to bring about change in listeners.

The Director's Role

A good speakers' bureau director will be a benevolent dictator. The director must be benevolent because the bureau is run not for the director but for the larger aims of the organization and because the bureau depends on volunteers who give their services out of a sense of conviction and duty. The director must be a sort of dictator because a bureau can get out of hand if it is not properly managed.

A director needs to pay particular attention to the assignment of speakers. The right speaker should be assigned to each speech to make sure speaking resources are employed to best advantage. The director should make sure that the better speakers are not overworked. No bureau member should be authorized to accept an invitation to represent the organization. All invitations should be forwarded to the director, who then decides who speaks to whom.

Pattern Speeches. Most of the facts speakers need can be furnished in the form of a pattern speech, a generic talk written for a hypothetical speaker to deliver to a hypothetical audience. The bureau director should have the responsibility for seeing that each speaker is supplied with an official pattern talk for each speech on the bureau's list. Although most speakers should speak from notes and all speakers should adapt each talk to the situation, the pattern talk remains a valuable aid. It should serve as a model of organization, it can guide a speaker in choosing language to express ideas.

The pattern talk also serves as a guide to organizational policy. Speakers need to be aware of any area where they might create confusion by speaking carelessly on policy, and in such an area they should follow the pattern talk closely.

Because pattern talks can rapidly get out of date, the bureau director should supply supplementary material on a regular basis. One common practice is to give each member of the bureau all the pattern talks in a binder. New data can then be mailed to everyone with instructions for the fresh information to be filed in the binder with the appropriate speech. Speakers should be encouraged to save and share relevant information they discover on their own.

Pattern talks will have to be rewritten periodically, and sometimes a speech outlives its usefulness to the point that it has to be pulled from the program.

Visual and Audio Aids. Speakers can be expected to supply only some of their audio and visual aids. Furnishing aids to speakers must be taken into account when planning the budget and staff of a bureau because it can be a major operation. Some aids must be available in multiple sets to make it possible for two or more speeches in large bureaus to be given simultaneously and to accommodate speakers who travel long distances from headquarters and might not be able to return material for several days.

Providing most of the visual aids gives the bureau director another control mechanism to make sure both the quality and content of the aids meet the organization's standards. Any charts and slides should have a professional look to avoid making speakers appear amateurish in their presentations.

Audience Analysis. Although speakers should be urged to conduct their own individual audience analysis, the director has the responsibility of seeing that the job is accomplished. It may be wise for the director to supply initial basic data on the audience such as size, age range, sex make-up, and other basic demographic information. The director should also supply forms that suggest other details the speakers must attempt to uncover, such as level of audience knowledge and listener attitude toward the topic of the speech. The material presented in chapter 3 will be useful in constructing a guide to proper audience analysis.

Feedback. A speakers' bureau director should be forthright in the effort to collect feedback from audiences. Speakers should aid in this effort, but at least part of the feedback, that which evaluates the effectiveness of the speakers, should go directly to the bureau director.

The speaker should be provided with a feedback form for each speech and should be instructed to fill it out as soon as possible after the speech. Where possible, the feedback should be recorded on the same day the speech is delivered. The speaker should be asked to give a report on the response of the audience during the speech to attempt to gauge the degree of interest in the subject and the extent to which the speaker was successful in informing, stimulating, convincing, or actuating the group. The form should include space for the speaker to list in detail questions the listeners asked. Any other useful information gathered in conversations before or after the speech should also be recorded. The speaker should supply an accurate count of the number of people who attended the speech, along with any notations about persons of special importance who were present.

A speaker evaluation form filled out by selected members of an audience can be used in a variety of ways. For some speeches, a spot check is all that is required, and a single evaluation form may be supplied to the person in charge of the program. For other speakers and speeches, the director may decide that a larger sample should be used, and the organization can be asked to have all the officers or even all the members fill out the form. Most audiences will cooperate in this effort, but there could be some groups where discretion would dictate that no request for evaluation be made.

The evaluation form can request information on delivery of the speech or on its impact on the audience, or both types of information can be requested.

A checklist on delivery might ask that the speaker be rated on a scale of perhaps 1 to 5 (excellent to adequate) on such items as physical behavior and voice, clarity of organization, effectiveness of language, and impressiveness of content.

A rough scale can be constructed to get an approximate idea of how the speech affected the audience. For example, the form might ask, "How do you feel about the ideas advanced in the speech: strongly agree—mildly agree—neutral—mildly disagree—strongly disagree," "Did this speech cause you to change your attitude toward the [speaker's organization]: very positive change—slight positive change—no change—slight negative change—very negative change," or "Following the speech, did you feel you understood [the organization's] position: a lot better—a little better—the same—less well—much less well."

Speaker's Kit. Some material can be provided to the speakers in a folder the speakers should keep on file. The pattern speeches and the updated material should go in this speaker's kit. It should include the audience analysis forms and samples of forms used to evaluate the speaker. It might be expanded to include a list of tips on delivery and suggestions on handling the Q&A.

Publicity. The bureau and its speeches should be advertised. Where appropriate, press coverage should be sought for speeches. This may be especially beneficial in smaller towns or rural areas. The bureau itself must be publicized at least in its initial stages. In addition to soliciting help from employees in making the bureau known, the director should attempt to draw up a list of current officers or other contacts in target groups to construct a mailing list for speaker bureau brochures. In some cases, a display set up in lobbies or other public places can advertise the bureau.

Record Keeping. Bureau directors should maintain a log of bureau activities. The log should make it easy for the director to prepare a detailed quarterly or annual report indicating the number of audiences the bureau reached and the total number of listeners who heard the speeches. This information may be especially useful if it breaks the audiences down by types and relates the types of audiences to the various messages the speakers are presenting.

Such a record enables the director to tell at a glance which speakers are overworked and which need to be exhorted to do more. It also suggests the level of demand for the bureau to guide the director in recruiting new speakers.

All press releases, evaluation forms, and letters of appreciation should be retained to help provide a basis for justification of the bureau's existence.

Reinforcing Speakers

Speakers need to be encouraged in their efforts and recognized for the time and energy they put into a speakers' program. Research has shown one rather surprising instance of positive reinforcement that comes from speaking. It has been discovered that, to some degree, speakers persuade themselves as they speak. By repeating the arguments for a corporate position over and over, a speaker comes to believe even more strongly in the case being made.

Other kinds of support must come from the speaker's organization. Only rarely are speaker bureau members paid for their efforts, and in some cases they are not even fully reimbursed for all their expenses. But even when speakers do get money for speaking, the amounts are usually modest and cannot be expected to supply adequate motivation for the extra work involved in making speeches. Most bureaus find it advisable to offer additional incentive.

Awards. From lapel pins to certificates to gold watches, speakers' bureau directors find ways to reward speakers. In some cases, everyone gets the same recognition for membership in the bureau. In others, the awards may offer varying degrees of recognition based on length of service or number of speeches. Sometimes a letter of commendation from the chief executive officer of the organization can supplement the award system.

Newsletters. A regular form of communication from the bureau director to the speakers can be one means of reinforcement. A speakers' bureau newsletter can serve to encourage speakers by reporting what other members of the bureau are doing. A newsletter may include useful tips, sometimes supplied by bureau members. It can report the kinds of questions audiences are asking, it can carry news on fresh information being supplied for the speeches, and it can contain humor to keep spirits up.

Banquets. An annual or semiannual luncheon or dinner meeting may be an excellent way to reinforce speakers in their work. Personal encouragement from top management can be delivered in such a setting, and a speaker can be brought in to address some of the issues considered in the bureau speeches. The banquet offers an ideal opportunity for award presentations to speakers.

The Professional Speaker

Sometimes an organization's message can best be delivered by a speaker who is paid to do the job on either a full- or part-time basis. Celebrities are sometimes hired for this purpose; an actor or an athlete who is widely known can become a popular speaker. In some cases, experts from the academic world, especially in the areas of economics or science, have a slight edge over a regular employee. Of course, an employee could be hired for the purpose of making speeches, or employees with considerable speaking ability or special areas of expertise could be assigned as full-time speakers for a specified period.

In spite of the many advantages of the hired gun approach to speech making, it has one major disadvantage: the hired speaker does not have the extra boost in credibility that comes from a person who can say, "I'm doing this over and above my regular duties because I think it's important for you to get this message."

Training Speakers' Bureau Members

A speakers' bureau should attract persons with better-than-average speaking skills. Even so, training is almost always a good idea.

Some bureau members may have learned to speak in one of the "how to be confident in front of an audience" schools. As a result, they may be making serious mistakes in a highly confident manner. But even good speakers should benefit from a review of speech techniques. In addition, a training session helps build *esprit de corps* among bureau members. And such training gives the director a chance to see the speakers in action, to assess the ways in which each speaker can best be used, and to determine if some speakers should be eliminated from the program.

A training program also permits a reasonable degree of control over policy. The individual changes speakers make in the pattern talks can be monitored to make certain no major errors are committed. Since more than one speaker may be speaking on the same topic in training, speakers can see the subject from a perspective other than their own.

Speakers also benefit by having the opportunity for a dry run before they face an outside audience. Even experienced speakers will appreciate the practice as an opportunity to try out a new talk or experiment with changes in one they have given before.

The ideal training session will be limited to speakers' bureau members and will be designed to prepare them to deliver a bureau speech. This type of training focuses on the needs of the bureau in a way that will not be possible in training from Toastmasters, a college night class, or a professional speech training firm with a fixed program. The alternatives are better than no training at all, but they should not be the speaker bureau director's preferred solution.

In-house trainers can be used if qualified staff members are available. This approach will be the best for policy control and will probably be the least expensive type of training.

If an outside trainer is used, some guidelines are useful in setting up the program:

1. Insist on training that includes both theory and practice. Either extreme should be avoided. If a trainer does nothing more than listen to speeches and evaluate them, the speakers will gain little in the way of principles they can apply to other speeches. On the other hand, a series of lectures on the techniques of speaking will be of relatively little value if they are not put into practice and critiqued.

2. Insist that the trainer know and support the objectives of the bureau. Any trainer who does not insist on seeing pattern speeches in advance and does not make careful inquiries about the nature of the speaking program should be suspect from the start. Any trainer who is condescending should not be hired.

3. Insist that the trainer supply references. References should be demanded and checked.

4. Insist on monitoring the training. The training should be observed by the director

or the director's representative at least the first few times. Often it is a good idea to have sessions open to higher management so the progress of the training can be seen first-hand. A training session should serve both to build speaking skills and to prepare communications staff personnel to either conduct the training themselves or to be better prepared to observe and evaluate speakers in the field.

5. Insist on program evaluation. Each speaker should fill out a critique of the training, with special emphasis on finding out how the training affected the speaker's performance.

6. Insist on relevant content. Some speech trainers spend too much time on such relatively unimportant areas as voice quality and standard pronunciation. Do not employ an out-of-work elocutionist to train a modern speaker.

If a director must choose between training a large number of speakers in a shallow program or training a smaller number in a thorough program, the second alternative should be selected. A director will usually be better off with a few well-trained speakers than with greater numbers of speakers inadequately prepared for their job.

A Model Program

A training model that has been used successfully many times involves ten to twelve participants in three days of lecture-discussions and exercises. The material covered in the lecture-discussions includes speech delivery, audience analysis, speech objectives, patterns of organization, using evidence to support ideas, oral language and semantics, handling the Q&A, and persuasion.

Half of the time is used for explanation of these topics and discussion of their application. The other half is devoted to four speaking exercises. The exercises consist of a warm-up talk (three to five minutes), a model miniature speech (five to seven minutes), a speech introducing another participant's speech (one to three minutes), and a dress rehearsal of a bureau speech (fifteen to twenty minutes). All speeches are recorded on videotape and played back for evaluation. The last speech is opened to questions by the participants, who play the role of the audience designated by the speaker. That speech and its critique require the entire third day of the program.

Follow-up Training

After a speaker has been a member of a bureau for two or three years, follow-up training will usually be advisable. Less time might be devoted to formal lecture or discussion in this training, with more emphasis spent on critique of performance. A speaker might, for example, be asked to repeat a recent speech, which would be taped and evaluated.

This type of training can be done in small groups or conducted on a one-to-one basis. In some instances, it can be accomplished by having a staff member sit in on a speech and build the training around observations of the speaker's performance.

Follow-up training polishes skills, reinforces speakers by reminding them that the organization still cares about their performance, and serves to check on any possible deviations from policy that may have crept into speeches.

MORE SOPHISTICATED MEASUREMENT OF SPEECH RESULTS

In the case of a major speech by an executive or an occasional speakers' bureau talk, it may be useful to measure the change in an audience more precisely than would be possible with any method discussed so far. The services of a professional polling agency are required for such a measurement.

Increasingly communicators responsible for speaking programs may discover that demands for greater productivity apply to their work. The mere counting of the number of speeches, speakers, audiences, and topics covered may not provide adequate proof of a program's success.

Some speech writers have the mistaken notion that the effect of speeches cannot be accurately determined. That is not the case. The effect of a speech can be measured, but the effort—and the cost—will be considerable.

The greater problem is that of deciding in advance what the speech communication program should accomplish. If the program aims to change attitudes, attitudes can be measured before and after the speech to determine the extent of the change. If the program aims to raise the level of information, the increase in what an audience knows after a speech, if any, can be tested.

A professional polling organization could, for example, telephone a representative sample of the membership of a major civic group prior to a speech and establish the level of opinion or information at that time. Follow-up polls of people who heard the speech could establish the change with a specified degree of accuracy.

PRESS COVERAGE

In some instances, as in a major political address, a speaker may aim for an audience far broader than the listeners present at the speech. Such a speech reaches and affects its prime audience through the news media. Even in the case of speeches where the most important audience is the one physically present, additional press coverage may be valuable.

Given the small amount of space or time likely to be afforded a typical speech by the media, it is realistic to expect that little of the substance of a talk will be reported. Indeed, because of the need of most reporters for a lead, a news story may often appear distorted from the speech writer's perspective. Except in rare instances, speech writers should expect the speaking event to get more coverage than the material in the speech.

This kind of publicity can still be useful. It advertises the speaking program, it may get a little of the message over, and it will probably be a boost to the speaker's ego.

Major speeches usually deserve a press release. Opinions differ on this matter, but providing the press with an advance copy of the speech will often be beneficial. The advance copy is especially important if television coverage is expected because the script becomes the guide for deciding what part of the speech to put on tape.

THE SPEECH AFTER DELIVERY

Several years ago, the head of Exxon gave a speech at Rutgers University in which he spoke forcefully on the preservation of private enterprise. Exxon's public affairs department decided to print 100,000 copies of the speech for distribution to people it had targeted as a good secondary audience for the speech. The copies were mailed with a "hang-on," a small card signed by the vice-president for public affairs.

The mailing elicited nearly 800 letters with requests for 30,000 additional copies. Fifteen requests for the right to reprint the speech were received from publications with a total circulation of 700,000. The letters came from a great variety of sources, including 100 college professors, 20 other oil companies, and 14 chambers of commerce. Only 17 of the letters were unfavorable.

Economist John Kenneth Galbraith was on the original target audience list, and he wrote a review attacking the speech in the *New York Times Book Review*. As a result, Exxon received another wave of requests for copies, many of them from people who felt that if Galbraith disliked the speech, it must be good. A negative notice of the speech appeared in Milton Moskowitz's nationally syndicated column. It too resulted in a number of requests for reprints.

Exxon finally printed 150,000 copies of the address. Although the Rutgers speech response was not at all typical of the reaction to the six to eight speeches Exxon annually reprinted at that time, the coordinator of creative services in the public affairs department, Otto W. Glade, summarized his feelings on the reprinting of speeches by saying, "It's additional mileage and for us it has been a worthwhile venture" (Glade 1975, 20-22).

Target Audience

Keeping an up-to-date mailing list for reprinted speeches can be a problem, and the costs can be considerable. But in a least some cases, the reprint can be added with little extra expense to mail already going to such groups as stockholders or employees. Special attention should be paid to mailing reprints to sources likely to reprint it: distant newspapers that would not have covered the speech, political figures who might quote the speech or include it in the *Congressional Record*, and the editor of *Vital Speeches*, among others.

A few special comments on *Vital Speeches* may be in order. This twice-a-week publication containing ten to twelve speeches per issue is the most widely read compilation of speeches in North America. It is found in all major libraries. *Vital Speeches* seeks to print speeches as they were delivered (it carried President Carter's slip of the tongue in his Democratic National Convention speech in 1980 as "Hubert Horatio Hornblower Humphrey"). The editor therefore does not usually alter copy, and a typographical error in a speech manuscript will be printed.

Because the *Vital Speeches* format includes a title and a subtitle, a brief digression on titles of speeches may be in order. Traditionally speeches, unlike written communications, have not had titles. Titles are after-thoughts. No one knew at the time that Lincoln was delivering "The Gettysburg Address" or that Patrick Henry was giving a speech to be called "Give Me Liberty or Give Me Death." But titles are necessary for publication and occasionally are required for printed programs in advance of a meeting. A title should serve two functions: it should catch attention, and it should concisely express the subject of the talk. The title plus subtitle enables a writer to accomplish both objectives.

It would be unfair to say that *Vital Speeches* ignores the quality of speeches, but the failure of the editor to print a speech submitted should not be taken by the writer as a mark of failure. The publication will carry most major political speeches, and if the number of speeches available is great, some good speeches will not be published. *Vital Speeches* favors current material and is unlikely to use a speech after several months have passed.

Format

The standard format for printed speeches seems to be the 3½ × 8½ inch pamphlet designed to fit in a regular business envelope. Only a few variations on this format are seen. Perhaps because organizations do not wish to appear to be spending a lot of money on reprints, many are rather dull and unattractive in appearance. Some efforts to enliven reprints include adding a picture of the speaker, highlighting quotations from the speech on the inside cover, attaching a few samples of the Q&A at the end, and using artwork on the cover. More effort could be paid to this matter.

The "hang-on" Exxon used is basically a special type of business card included with the talk to indicate who sent it. An address printed on the pamphlet is a good idea since it won't get lost and will aid anyone who wants to write for reprints.

Other Uses of a Speech after Delivery

Small radio stations often use taped excerpts from speeches. A videotape of a speech can be made to show to employees or other interested groups. A small number of audiotapes or videotapes may be mailed in place of printed speeches. This will not be a frequent practice, but some tapes of this sort do circulate because of such factors as the speaker's outstanding delivery, the use of especially interesting visual aids, or the presence of certain types of humor that are better heard than read.

However weary a writer may be after a speech has finally been completed, the idea of doing something more with it should be given careful consideration. All that work should not always end up in a file drawer.

CONCLUSION

Although we live in a highly sophisticated communication environment, old-fashioned public speaking still has impact. The days of Babbittry, if they ever truly existed at all, are over; the speech deserves to be treated as a major weapon in the communication arsenal of any organization with a message to deliver. A live speaker before a live audience remains a vital force, and the record of the encounter between the two, in print or on tape, may extend the influence of the speech even more.

Appendix: Speech Writing Resources

PUBLICATIONS

Delaney, R. E. *The Executive Speech Maker*. Quarterly publication of the Clearing House for Speech Humor, Box 15259, Wedgewood, Seattle, Washington 98115.

Orben, Robert. *Orben's Current Comedy*. The Comedy Center, 700 Orange Street, Wilmington, Delaware 19801.

Vital Speeches of the Day can be found in almost any library. It is published twice monthly by the City News Publishing Company, Box 1247, Mount Pleasant, South Carolina 29464.

Newsletters published for speech writers are *Speechwriter's Newsletter*, Ragan Communications, 407 South Dearborn, Chicago, Illinois 60605, and *Executive Speaker*, Box 292437, Dayton, Ohio 45429.

CONSULTANTS

Management consultants who specialize in the market for speech writers include Jean Cardwell, Cardwell Consultants, Box 59418, Chicago, Illinois 60659; Bill Cantor, The Cantor Concern, 171 Madison Avenue, New York, New York 10016; Larry Marshall, Marshall Consultants, Inc., 360 East 65th Street, New York, New York 10021; and Wesley Poriotis, Wesley-Brown & Bartle, 152 Madison Avenue, New York, New York, 10016 (with branch offices in Chicago and Washington, D.C.).

ORGANIZATIONS

International Association of Business Communicators, 870 Market Street, San Francisco, California 94102. Its publication, *Communication World*, features occasional material on speech writing.

National Association of Corporate Speaker Activities, Jada Banks, C&P Telephone, 609 East Grace Street, Richmond, VA 23219. For speech writers, speakers' bureau directors, consultants, and trainers.

Public Relations Society of America, 845 Third Avenue, New York, New York 10022. The *Public Relations Journal* is known as one of the finest communications journals in the U.S.

TRAINING

Speech writing seminars are offered by, among others, Jeff Cook, 2425 Fifth Avenue West, Seattle, Washington 98119; James Fox, the dean of speech writing trainers, through New York University and the Public Relations Society of America, Madison Avenue, Room 1412, New York, New York 10017; Larry Ragan Communications, 407 South Dearborn, Chicago, Illinois 60605; Fraser Seitel, Professional Development Institute, 242 West Thirty-eighth Street, Room 500, New York, New York 10018; and Jerry Tarver, Box 444, University of Richmond, Virginia 23173.

AIDS

Fettig, Art. *Humorize Your Speeches*. Ad-Tapes, Post Office Box 66, Palos Verdes Estates, California 90274.

Gliner, Art. *Humor Workshop* Audiotape. The Humor Communication Company, 8521 Grubb Road, 101, Silver Spring, Maryland 20910.

The Script-Master(TM) speech portfolio is available from Brewer-Cantelmo Co., 116 East Twenty-seventh Street, New York, New York 10016. The portfolio provides a handy and attractive means for the speaker to carry a manuscript to the lectern.

Bibliography

Anchell, Melvin. "A Psychoanalytic Look at Homosexuality." *Vital Speeches of the Day* (February 15, 1986).

Anderson, W. S. "Keynote Address." A Speech before the Conference on Technology Transfer, Washington, D.C., December 7, 1977.

Auer, J. Jeffery. "Who Writes Parliamentary Speeches? Political Speechwriting in England." Paper read at the Annual Convention of the Central States Speech Association, Chicago, Illinois, April 11, 1981.

Avery, William T. "Roman Ghost-Writers." *Classical Journal* 54 (1959).

Baeder, Donald L. "Chemical Waste: Fact versus Perception." *Vital Speeches of the Day* (June 1, 1980).

Baskin, Otis. "Speech Writing—A Major Public Relations Activity?" Paper presented at the Annual Meeting of the American Academy of Advertising, Newport, Rhode Island, April 1974.

Bays, Karl D. "Changing Health Care Practices." *Vital Speeches of the Day* (January 1, 1986).

Bender, James F. *NBC Handbook of Pronunciation.* New York: Thomas Y. Crowell Company, 1943.

Billups, Rufus L. "Black History: Torch for the Future." *Vital Speeches of the Day* (September 15, 1979).

Blair, Hugh. *Lectures on Rhetoric and Belles Lettres.* London: Strahan and Cadell, 1793.

Bolger, William F. "The Postal Services: Success or Failure?" *Vital Speeches of the Day* (February 1, 1980).

Bonee, John R. "The Care and Feeding of the Executive Speaker." *Vital Speeches of the Day* (January 15, 1982).

Bormann, Ernest G. "Ethics of Ghostwritten Speeches." *Quarterly Journal of Speech* (October 1961a).

————. "Ghostwriting Speeches—A Reply." *Quarterly Journal of Speech* (December 1961b).

Brigance, William Norwood. *Speech: Its Techniques and Disciplines in a Free Society.* 2d ed. New York: Appleton-Century-Crofts, 1961.

Buckley, Robert J. "Management Short-Fall in the 1980's: A Threat for the American Economy." *Vital Speeches of the Day* (February 1, 1980).

Burson-Marsteller. *The Executive Speechmaker: A Systems Approach.* New York: Foundation for Public Relations Research and Education, 1980.

————. "The Chief Executive and the Corporate Credibility Gap," *Burson-Marsteller Report* (February 1975).

Busse, James G. "Ghostwriters in the Executive Suite." *TWA Ambassador* (June 1978).

Butler, Owen. "Television Can Show and Tell, But Can It Listen?" *Vital Speeches of the Day* (August 1, 1981).

Caldwell, John L. "American Purpose and International Human Rights." *Vital Speeches of the Day* (February 1, 1980).

Capen, Richard G. "Generating Good Signs." *Vital Speeches of the Day* (October 1, 1980).

Cecil, Andrew R. "Independence and World Citizenship." *Vital Speeches of the Day* (August 1, 1980).

Chang, Mei-Jung, and Charles R. Gruner. "Audience Reaction to Self-Disparaging Humor." *Southern Speech Communication Journal* (Summer 1981).

Chisholm, Shirley. "Vote for the Individual, Not the Political Party." *Vital Speeches of the Day* (August 15, 1978)

Costello, John. "Jests Can Do Justice to Your Speeches." *Nation's Business* (January 1978).

Cox, LaWanda and John H. "Andrew Johnson and His Ghost Writers: An Analysis of the Freedmen's Bureau and Civil Rights Veto Message." *Mississippi Valley Historical Review* 48 (1961).

Crutchfield, Edward. "Profitable Banking in the 1980's." *Vital Speeches of the Day* (June 15, 1980).

Cuomo, Mario M. "Your One Life Can Make a Difference." *Vital Speeches of the Day* (July 15, 1985).

Dayton, Kenneth N. "The Case for Corporate Philanthropy." *Vital Speeches of the Day* (August 1, 1980).

Dee, Robert F. "Musical Glasses and the Milky Way." Address delivered to the Fourth Franklin Conference, Philadelphia, November 23, 1979.

Detz, Joan. *How to Write and Give a Speech.* New York: St. Martin's Press, 1984.

Devlin, L. Patrick. "The Influences of Ghostwriting on Rhetorical Criticism." *Today's Speech* (Number 3, 1974).

Ehninger, Douglas, Bruce E. Gronbeck, and Alan H. Monroe. *Principles of Speech Communication.* 8th ed. Glenview, Ill.: Scott, Foresman and Company, 1980.

Eller, Karl. "Miracle in a Glass: The Free Enterprise System." *Vital Speeches of the Day* (February 1, 1979).

Enos, Richard L. "The Persuasive and Social Force of Logography in Ancient Greece." *Central States Speech Journal* 25 (1974).

Fallows, James. "The Passionless Presidency." *Atlantic* (May 1979, June 1979).

Fippinger, Grace. "This Is a Very Good Time." *Vital Speeches of the Day* (January 15, 1980).

Freshley, Dwight L. "Gubernatorial Ghost Writers." *Southern Speech Journal* (Winter 1965).

Glade, Otto W. "Getting Additional Mileage Out of That Speech." *Journal of Organizational Communication* 4 (1975).

Golden, James L. "John F. Kennedy and the 'Ghosts.' " *Quarterly Journal of Speech* 52 (1966).

Gould, Charles. "Stop Tampering with the Machinery." *Vital Speeches of the Day* (February 1, 1980).

Grace, J. Peter. "The Problem of Big Government." *Vital Speeches of the Day* (May 1, 1985).

Gray, Harry J. "The Essential American Virtues." *Vital Speeches of the Day* (June 15, 1984).

Grayson, Melvin J. "Ghosts at the Podium." *Advertising Age* (October 9, 1978).

_____. "The Last Best Hope: Words." *Vital Speeches of the Day* (July 15, 1981).

Hanley, John. "Lessons I've Learned since Graduation." *Vital Speeches of the Day* (July 15, 1981).

_____. "Why Ban Reason from the Consumer Safety Debate?" *Vital Speeches of the Day* (August 1, 1977).

Honan, William H. "The Men behind Nixon's Speeches." *New York Times Magazine* (January 19, 1969).

Horton, Thomas R. "Winning in the Global Marketplace." *Vital Speeches of the Day* (April 15, 1986).

Huskey, Ken W. *Spokesperson*. Palm Springs: K. W. Huskey Associates, 1980.

Iacocca, Lee. "We're Taxing Our Own Kids." *Vital Speeches of the Day* (March 15, 1985).

Jebb, R. C. *Attic Orators*. London: Macmillan, 1876.

Jones, Reginald H. "The Reputation of Business." *Vital Speeches of the Day* (February 1, 1986).

Jones, Barrie. "The Understanding of Scale." *Vital Speeches of the Day* (January 15, 1980).

Kelley, Joseph J., Jr. *Speechwriting: The Master Touch*. Harrisburg: Stackpole Books, 1980.

Kendall, Donald M. "The Four Simple Truths of Management." *Vital Speeches of the Day* (May 15, 1986).

Kennedy, George. *The Art of Persuasion in Greece*. Princeton: Princeton University Press, 1963.

Kilpatrick, James Jackson. *Richmond News-Leader* (September 12, 1981).

Klappa, Gale E. "Journalism and the Anti-Media Backlash." *Vital Speeches of the Day* (April 1, 1985).

Kodak. *How to be a Knockout with AV!* Eastman Kodak Company Publicaton S-31. Rochester, N.Y.: Kodak, 1984.

_____. *Presenting Yourself*. Eastman Kodak Company Publication S-60. Rochester, N.Y.: Kodak, 1982.

_____. *Slides: Planning and Producing Slide Programs*. Eastman Kodak Company

Publication S-30. Rochester, N.Y.: Kodak, 1984.

———. *Speechmaking . . . More than Words Alone.* Eastman Kodak Company Publication S-25. Rochester, N.Y.: Kodak, 1979.

Lamm, Richard D. "Time to Change Course." *Vital Speeches of the Day* (October 15, 1985).

Lichacz, Janine A. "The Art of Corporate Speech Writing: Trends and Techniques." Master's thesis, Fairfield University, 1980.

Loden, Marilyn. "Networking: It Can Change Your Life." *Vital Speeches of the Day* (August 1, 1981).

Love, Howard M. "Reindustrialization: Friend or Foe?" *Vital Speeches of the Day* (January 15, 1981).

Lovell, W. M. "How to Shape a Speech—From Invitation to Podium." *Journal of Organizational Communication* 2 (1978).

Lynch, Dudley. "It's Time We Give the Brain Its Due." *Journal of Organizational Communication* 1 (1981).

McCormick, Richard D. "Business Loves English." *Vital Speeches of the Day* (November 1, 1984).

McDonald, John B. "Speechwriting." In *Inside Public Relations.* Edited by Bill Cantor. New York: Longman, 1984.

———. Washington Post (January 1, 1977).

MacDonald, Robert W. "A Farewell to Arms in Financial Services." *Vital Speeches of the Day* (April 15, 1985).

McGillicuddy, John F. "The Economy, Energy and the President's Proposals." *Vital Speeches of the Day* (September 15, 1979).

McGlon, Charles A. "How I Prepare My Sermons: A Symposium." *Quarterly Journal of Speech* 40 (February 1954).

Mahoney, David. "National Issues and Consumer Attitudes." *Vital Speeches of the Day* (July 1, 1978).

Marotta, George. "Stock Market Message." *Vital Speeches of the Day* (March 1, 1986).

May, Ernest R. "Ghost Writing and History." *American Scholar* 22 (1953).

Mullins, James P. "What's So Wrong with 'The Military Industrial Complex'?" *Vital Speeches of the Day* (December 15, 1983).

Newell, Sara A., and Thomas King. "The Keynote Address of the Democratic National Convention, 1972: The Evolution of a Speech." *Southern Speech Communication Journal* 39 (1974).

Nichols, Marie Hochmuth. *Rhetoric and Criticism.* Baton Rouge: Louisiana State University Press, 1963.

Nizer, Louis. *Thinking on Your Feet; Adventures in Speaking.* Garden City, N.Y.: Doubleday, 1944.

Oliver, Robert T. "Syngman Rhee: A Case Study in Transnational Oratory." *Quarterly Journal of Speech* 48 (1962).

Ong, John D. "The U.S. Tire Industry in the 1980's." *Vital Speeches of the Day* (December 1, 1980).

Orben, Robert. *4 Ways to Improve Your Public Speaking.* Wilmington, Del.: Comedy Center, 1982.

Ostar, Allan W. "Higher Education for a New Era," *Vital Speeches of the Day* (February 1, 1980).

Ott, John. *How to Write and Deliver a Speech*. New York: Cornerstone Library, 1976.

Pearson, Lester B. "The Four Faces of Peace." Nobel Peace Prize Acceptance Speech, Oslo, Norway, 1957.

Perlis, Leo. "Organized Labor Needs a Facelift." *Vital Speeches of the Day* (September 15, 1984).

Perrett, Gene. "Humor Is Serious Business." *Vital Speeches of the Day* (August 15, 1985).

Persico, Joseph E. "The Rockefeller Rhetoric: Writing Speeches for the 1970 Campaign." *Today's Speech* 20 (Spring 1972).

Peterson, Peter G. "The Oil and Debt and Poverty Emergence of the Eighties." *Vital Speeches of the Day* (December 15, 1980).

Pickens, Judy E. *Without Bias*. New York: John Wiley & Sons, 1982.

Pope, Jean. "Care and Feeding of Speechwriters." *Public Relations Journal* 35 (May 1979).

Poriotis, Wesley. "Is There Life after Manuscript?" *Public Relations Journal* 37 (July 1981).

Potter, Norman D. "Leadership: The Need for Renaissance." *Vital Speeches of the Day* (January 1, 1980).

Reagan, Ronald. "Inaugural Address." *Vital Speeches of the Day* (February 15, 1981).

_____. "The Elements of Peace." *Vital Speeches of the Day* (December 1, 1985).

Regan, Donald T. "The Tax Reform Issue." *Vital Speeches of the Day* (May 1, 1984).

Reichardt, Carl E. "Does Two Plus Two Equal Five?" *Vital Speeches of the Day* (September 15, 1981).

Rockefeller, David. "The Chief Executive in the Year 2000." *Vital Speeches of the Day* (January 1, 1980).

Rooney, Andy. *Richmond Times-Dispatch* (July 8, 1980).

Rosenbaum, Ron. "Who Puts the Words in the President's Mouth?" *Esquire* (December 1985).

Rosenman, Samuel I. *Working with Roosevelt*. New York: Harper and Brothers, 1952.

Safire, William. *Before the Fall*. New York: Tower Publications, 1975.

_____. *Full Disclosure*. New York: Ballantine Books, 1977.

_____. "Reagan Betrays a Lack of Homework." *Richmond Times-Dispatch* (June 19, 1981).

Senese, Donald J. "Capturing the Spirit of Educational Quality." *Vital Speeches of the Day* (May 1, 1985).

Shafer, Carl., ed. *Excellence in Teaching: With the Seven Laws*. Grand Rapids: Baker Book House, 1985.

Shannon, Thomas A. "Local Control of Schools." *Vital Speeches of the Day* (January 15, 1986).

Shapiro, Irving. "The Lawyer's Special Role." *Vital Speeches of the Day* (February 15, 1979).

Shrum, Robert. "No Private Smiles." *New Times* (June 11, 1976).

Silber, John R. "Of Mermaids and Magnificence." *Vital Speeches of the Day* (July 15, 1986).

Simonson, Brenda W. "Corporate Fitness Programs Pay Off." *Vital Speeches of the Day* (July 1, 1986).

Smith, Craig R. "Appendum to 'Contemporary Political Speech Writing.'" *Southern Speech Communication Journal* 42 (Winter 1977).

_____. "Contemporary Political Speech Writing." *Southern Speech Communication Journal* 42 (Fall 1976).

Smith, Donald K. "Ghostwritten Speeches." *Quarterly Journal of Speech* 47 (December 1961).

Smith, Roger B. "Humanities and Business." *Vital Speeches of the Day* (August 1, 1984).

Smith, Terry C. *Making Successful Presentations.* New York: John Wiley & Sons, 1984).

Sorensen, Theodore C. *Decision-Making in the White House.* New York: Columbia University Press, 1963.

Staley, D. C. "Can We Get There from Here?" *Vital Speeches of the Day* (November 1, 1980).

Stewart, D. Michael. "The Changing of the Guard." *Vital Speeches of the Day* (August 15, 1985).

Tarver, Jerry. "Can't Nobody Here Use This Language?" *Vital Speeches of the Day* (May 1, 1979).

_____. "Communication and Credibility." *Vital Speeches of the Day* (April 15, 1981).

_____. "The Speech Writer in University Relations." *Case Currents* 9 (February (1983).

_____. "Making a Speech in a Different Culture." *Communication World* 1 (February 1984).

Taylor, Anita. "Women as Leaders." *Vital Speeches of the Day* (May 1, 1984).

Teresa, Mother. "The Gift of Peace." *Vital Speeches of the Day* (June 1, 1980).

Thatcher, Margaret. "Britain: International Relations." *Vital Speeches of the Day* (March 15, 1985).

Toot, Joseph F. "The Lost and Crucial Art." *Vital Speeches of the Day* (February 1, 1980).

Tower, Raymond C. "Government Regulation: Slow Death for Free Enterprise." *Vital Speeches of the Day* (September 1, 1980).

Usher, S. "Lysias and His Clients." *Greek, Roman, and Byzantine Studies* 17 (1976).

Van Andel, Jay. "Business Leadership against Inflation." *Vital Speeches of the Day* (July 1, 1979).

Walker, George Lee. *The Chronicles of Doodah.* Boston: Houghton Mifflin, 1985.

Welsh, James J. *The Speech Writing Guide.* New York: John Wiley & Sons, 1968.

Wise, Paul S. "The Arson for Profit Business." *Vital Speeches of the Day* (November 1, 1978).

Woolsey, R. James. "Decision Making in Designing U.S. Naval Forces." *Vital Speeches of the Day* (July 1, 1978).

Index

About the Author

JERRY TARVER is Professor and Chairman of the Department of Speech Communication and Theatre Arts at the University of Richmond. He has conducted training in public speaking and speech writing for major corporations and government agencies throughout the United States and Canada. He is also co-author of *Communication in Business and the Professions* and the author of book chapters in *Inside Organizational Communication* and *Experts in Action*. His articles have appeared in such journals as *The Public Relations Journal* and *Communication World*, among others.